The Hidden Package

THE AZRIELI SERIES OF HOLOCAUST SURVIVOR MEMOIRS: PUBLISHED TITLES

ENGLISH TITLES

The Hidden Package

Claire Baum

THE AZRIELI FOUNDATION
www.azrielifoundation.org

Cover and book design by Mark Goldstein
Endpaper maps by Martin Gilbert
Map on page xxiii by François Blanc

LIBRARY AND ARCHIVES CANADA CATALOGUING IN PUBLICATION

Baum, Claire, 1936–, author
 The hidden package/ Claire Baum.

(The Azrieli series of Holocaust survivor memoirs; 6)
Includes bibliographical references and index.
ISBN 978-1-897470-47-3 (pbk.)

1. Baum, Claire, 1936–, – Childhood and youth. 2. Holocaust, Jewish (1939–1945) – Netherlands – Personal narratives. 3. Hidden children (Holocaust) – Netherlands – Biography. 4. Righteous Gentiles in the Holocaust – Netherlands – Biography. 5. Netherlands – History – German occupation, 1940–1945 – Biography. 6. Holocaust survivors – Canada – Biography. I. Azrieli Foundation, issuing body II. Title. III. Series: Azrieli series of Holocaust survivor memoirs. Series; VI

DS135.N6B38 2014   940.53'18092   C2014-905855-1

PRINTED IN CANADA

The Azrieli Series of Holocaust Survivor Memoirs

Naomi Azrieli, Publisher

Jody Spiegel, Program Director
Arielle Berger, Managing Editor
Matt Carrington, Editor
Devora Levin, Assistant Editor
Elizabeth Lasserre, Senior Editor, French-Language Editions
Elin Beaumont, Community and Education Initiatives
Catherine Person, Education and Academic Initiatives/French Editor
Stephanie Corazza, Academic and Education Initiatives
Marc-Olivier Cloutier, School and Education Initiatives
Elizabeth Banks, Digital Asset Curator and Archivist
Catherine Quintal, Digital Communications Assistant

Mark Goldstein, Art Director
François Blanc, Cartographer
Bruno Paradis, Layout, French-Language Editions

Contents

Series Preface:
In their own words...

In telling these stories, the writers have liberated themselves. For so many years we did not speak about it, even when we became free people living in a free society. Now, when at last we are writing about what happened to us in this dark period of history, knowing that our stories will be read and live on, it is possible for us to feel truly free. These unique historical documents put a face on what was lost, and allow readers to grasp the enormity of what happened to six million Jews — one story at a time.

David J. Azrieli, C.M., C.Q., M.Arch
Holocaust survivor and founder, The Azrieli Foundation

Since the end of World War II, approximately 40,000 Jewish Holocaust survivors have immigrated to Canada. Who they are, where they came from, what they experienced and how they built new lives for themselves and their families are important parts of our Canadian heritage. The Azrieli Foundation's Holocaust Survivor Memoirs Program was established in 2005 to preserve and share the memoirs written by those who survived the twentieth-century Nazi genocide of the Jews of Europe and later made their way to Canada. The memoirs encourage readers to engage thoughtfully and critically with the complexities of the Holocaust and to create meaningful connections with the lives of survivors.

Millions of individual stories are lost to us forever. By preserving the stories written by survivors and making them widely available to a broad audience, the Azrieli Foundation's Holocaust Survivor Memoirs Program seeks to sustain the memory of all those who perished at the hands of hatred, abetted by indifference and apathy. The personal accounts of those who survived against all odds are as different as the people who wrote them, but all demonstrate the courage, strength, wit and luck that it took to prevail and survive in such terrible adversity. The memoirs are also moving tributes to people — strangers and friends — who risked their lives to help others, and who, through acts of kindness and decency in the darkest of moments, frequently helped the persecuted maintain faith in humanity and courage to endure. These accounts offer inspiration to all, as does the survivors' desire to share their experiences so that new generations can learn from them.

The Holocaust Survivor Memoirs Program collects, archives and publishes select survivor memoirs and makes the print editions available free of charge to educational institutions and Holocaust-education programs across Canada. They are also available for sale online to the general public. All revenues to the Azrieli Foundation from the sales of the Azrieli Series of Holocaust Survivor Memoirs go toward the publishing and educational work of the memoirs program.

∽

The Azrieli Foundation would like to express appreciation to the following people for their invaluable efforts in producing this book: Mark Duffus (Maracle Inc.), Andrea Knight, Jason Logan, Therese Parent, and Margie Wolfe & Emma Rodgers of Second Story Press.

About the Glossary

The following memoir contains a number of terms, concepts and historical references that may be unfamiliar to the reader. For information on major organizations; significant historical events and people; geographical locations; religious and cultural terms; and foreign-language words and expressions that will help give context and background to the events described in the text, please see the glossary beginning on page 71.

Introduction

Claire Baum's extraordinary memoir, *The Hidden Package*, tells the important story of life and resistance in an occupied country during the Holocaust. Seeking to leave a legacy, she explores "what it was like to be a hidden child during World War II," and does so on multiple levels – from her perspective as a hidden child and from the standpoint of her biological parents and her wartime parents. There are several famous stories of hiding – *The Diary of Anne Frank* and Corrie Ten Boom's *The Hiding Place* are two well-known examples – yet it is both jolting and profoundly moving to read a direct account from those hidden. I felt a personal connection with Claire's story because my maternal grandparents, now long deceased, worked with the Dutch Resistance to hide Jewish families. Unfortunately, the details of their endeavours remain sketchy and my mother doesn't remember the names or faces of the various individuals and families her parents helped. Nonetheless, she clearly remembers that members of the Dutch Jewish community were well cared for by her mother and that they were safely hidden whenever the SS searched the house, which occurred as often as several times weekly, in a false floor between the first and second storeys, where the leather for her father's shoemaking shop was stored.[1]

---

1   Carolyne Van Der Meer, *Motherlode: A Mosaic of Dutch Wartime Experience* (Waterloo: Wilfrid Laurier University Press, 2014).

Claire Baum, in her moving account, tells us the other side of the story: what it was like to be the hidden. Claire and her sister, Ollie, found refuge with the Duchene family and, later, with Nel Van Woudenberg, whom they called "Tante Nel," for two-and-a-half years. They experienced some measure of stability during these unstable times, but for Claire and Ollie, remembering this time came at a price. When their wartime letters to their parents, Rudolph and Sophia Friedberg, were found some forty years later, the women had to confront their past, fully recognizing that seeing their handwritten "diary" would open a whole world that had, until then, remained deeply buried. Despite the fact that they kept in touch with Tante Nel until her death in 2006, some of what they experienced during that difficult time had been blocked out, no doubt both consciously and unconsciously.

This reaction is not surprising. Many child survivors worked hard to "forget" those years. Spending their energy looking forward, focusing on their new lives – especially those who left the Netherlands for Canada or elsewhere – they were able to immerse themselves in learning new customs, often a new language, and establishing themselves in a novel and faraway community. Claire avoided the trauma inherent in remembering her wartime experiences for years, but came to see the benefits to herself, survivors and the wider community – recording and speaking about one's past can help encourage education about tolerance, compassion, understanding and empathy.

Claire Baum's memoir makes it clear that even in the most painful and cruel situations, love and luck sometimes come through. Claire and Ollie were fortunate to be taken in by Tante Nel, who not only treated them as her own and gave them a safe haven, but also encouraged them to write to their parents, thus ensuring that they remained alive in their hearts and minds. Claire and Ollie were physically separated from their mother and father but they never questioned their love, which was inherent in their decision to hide the children separately, ensuring that they were as far out of harm's way as possible.

Even under lucky circumstances, the trauma experienced by many Jewish children as a result of having been hidden is significant. According to Dutch-Jewish child psychologist Dr. Bloeme Evers-Emden, who pioneered research into hidden children, the "psychological and practical consequences" on children were many and varied. Having to adapt to new surroundings and new people very quickly was tough on young children. Some were moved around multiple times and, due to mistrust, found it increasingly difficult to form attachments after the initial separation. When some children returned home, they had trouble reconnecting with their biological parents. As Evers-Emden writes, "Often the hidden children had had to change addresses several times, leading them to 'turn off their feelings' so as not to be overwhelmed by grief. After the war, many of them could not 'turn on' their feelings."[2]

Claire's parents did not speak to her about their past, yet they too must have suffered. Many parents of hidden children experienced "anticipated mourning" – a certainty that they or their children would be killed before they could reunite. Sometimes the biological parents could not "forgive" the "hiding-parents" for caring for their children. The "hiding-parents" also went through trauma, "suffering from grief after the child's departure."[3]

The decision to hide children was not one that any parent took lightly. Many factors added to the frightening possibility that there would be no reunion. One was the Jewish identity card, a document that the Nazi administration made mandatory by the end of 1941, decorated with a large black J that was impossible to erase. Neither Claire nor Ollie carried an identity card because they were both under the age of seven, but their parents certainly had the cards that marked

---

2 Bloeme Evers-Emden, "Hiding Jewish Children during World War II: The Psychological Aftermath," in *Jewish Political Studies Review* 19:1-2 (Spring 2007).

3 Ibid.

them for persecution. It was only because Claire's father participated in the resistance that he was able to secure false identity cards for himself and Claire's mother. Further considerations were finding a good place for the children – and money. In some cases, Dutch gentile families demanded compensation for hiding Jews seeking refuge. Sometimes, just a little money was required, but many families could not cover the costs.

The Friedbergs must have first considered whether it was even possible to find a hiding place for Claire and Ollie. In 1942, when Claire and Ollie went into hiding, there was not yet an organized underground network for hiding children in the Netherlands. Parents were frantic to find ways to protect their own. Anti-Jewish laws came into effect soon after the 1940 Nazi occupation and the Jewish community was the first large group to attempt to hide, but it was not until the second half of 1942 that organizations were formed to make safe refuge possible. The largest of these groups was the LO, or Landelijke Organisatie voor Hulp aan Onderduikers (National Organization for Help in Hiding), started by Orthodox Calvinist Church leader Reverend Slomp. The LO did not completely get off the ground until the fall of 1943, after most Dutch Jews had already been deported.[4] Although rescue operations were not set up in time to subvert the massive deportations of Jews – more than 100,000 between July 1942 and September 1943 were sent to the Westerbork transit camp, en route to Auschwitz and other death camps – by 1944, the resistance had organized efforts to hide more than 300,000 people, including approximately 30,000 Jews.[5] Many organizations contributed to the effort to hide Jews, but the LO had the greatest impact in terms of the sheer number of Jewish people it assisted. All told, organizations

---

4   Diane Wolf, *Beyond Anne Frank: Hidden Children and Postwar Families in Holland* (Berkeley: University of California Press, 2007).

5   Liesbeth van der Horst et al. *The Dutch Resistance Museum*. Verzetsmuseum Amsterdam, 2007.

and individuals were able to save more than 4,000 young lives during World War II.

Out of approximately 140,000 Jews living in the Netherlands in 1939 – a number that included some 25,000 Jewish-German refugees – 75 per cent were murdered during the course of the Holocaust.[6] Although the majority of Dutch Jewry did not survive the war, research done at Yad Vashem, the Holocaust museum and memorial, demonstrates that the Netherlands has one of the highest number of awards – 5,351 – for Righteous Among the Nations, a title given to those who risked their lives to save Jews during the war.[7]

And yet, Dutch citizens who dared to help were in the minority. One figure puts active resistance at less than 1 per cent.[8] This small percentage took extreme risks and lived with terrible uncertainty because they could not in good conscience abide by Nazi racial ideology or could not accept the volume of newly enforced laws. They were undeterred by fear and either found individual ways of helping to thwart Nazi rule or organized themselves into groups to do so.

Those who took in Jewish children took great risks, and not all truly understood what could happen to them if they were caught. The consequences were massive – arrests, deportations, even death. Betrayals by Nazi collaborators were common, as Claire and Ollie experienced in their first hiding place. Between 25,000 and 30,000 Jews went into hiding during the height of Nazi persecution; of those at least 12,000 were found out and did not survive.[9]

Thousands who did try to help, like the Duchene family, found their social circles affected, as their biological children could not talk about the new addition to the family and certainly could not bring

---

6 Wolf, *Beyond Anne Frank*.

7 http://www.yadvashem.org/yv/en/righteous/statistics.asp.

8 Mark Klempner, *The Heart Has Reasons* (Cleveland: The Pilgrim Press, 2006).

9 Marnix Croes, "The Holocaust in the Netherlands and the Rate of Jewish Survival," in *Holocaust and Genocide Studies*, Vol. 20: 3, pp. 474–499.

friends home from school. In fact, families subjected themselves to further risk by having any guests at all, so socializing was minimal.

The intense stress of the war was compounded for these war-time-parents. Resources such as food and clothing were limited and suddenly, there was another family "member" who needed both. The need to feed two extra mouths, particularly during the Hunger Winter – the 1944–45 famine Germany imposed on the western Netherlands by banning food transports to the area – was an enormous responsibility for Tante Nel. She would travel miles out of town on her bike to barter Claire and Ollie's old clothes for food. Moreover, her brother Pauw, who worked for the Resistance and had arranged for Claire and Ollie's stay with both the Duchene family and with his sister Nel, was at constant risk as a liaison between hidden families and the underground network.

In wartime, the layers of trauma grow like layers of new skin, and the end of the war brought relief only to some. Having lost their social networks because of the hidden children, most wartime-parents found themselves very much alone at war's end, without their pre-war friends and the hidden children they had grown to love. Biological parents, too, were deeply and negatively affected by their own experience of hiding. The effort required for them to adapt to their host family, always be friendly and polite, and never say what they felt or thought was significant, not to mention that they couldn't leave the house or even the very rooms in which they were hidden. In addition to the constant fear of being betrayed by someone on the outside, there were tensions over lack of control and authority inside the house. Further difficulties presented themselves as a result of the attachment – the love, even – that their hidden children had developed for the hiding-parents. Some biological parents were jealous and cut contact with the hiding-parents during difficult or dangerous times; others maintained the connection, developing larger family networks.

Some hidden children were so young that they forgot their Jewish names, as these had been suppressed. Others did not recognize their parents when they were reunited, and grew to view their wartime-parents as their real parents. Leaving them was therefore traumatic. Claire writes of her own reunion experience, "At first, we didn't want to go home with Mam and Pap, but how could we not? They had purposely sent us away to save our lives. They were separated from us all these years while they were hiding elsewhere; we couldn't break their hearts. When they hugged me, it was a familiar hug. I knew then they were our parents. I had missed their hugs and kisses for almost three years." Considering the extraordinary pressure Rudolph and Sophia Friedberg, Tante Nel and the girls were under, it is phenomenal that their strength, values and love for one another surmounted the challenges.

For some families, the challenges were made more difficult in August 1945, when the Dutch government passed a bill stating that resistance groups be consulted in determining the future of hidden children. Upon the bill becoming law, the government officially formed the Commissie voor Oorlogspleegkinderen or O P K (Commission for War Foster Children), which played a central role in preventing these children from being immediately returned to their parents. The law essentially allowed the state to sever parental rights, citing as reasons "abandonment or neglect."[10] Of course, Jewish parents had not abandoned or neglected their children but rather were attempting to save their lives by sending them into hiding. The law portrayed this as wilful abandonment.

Given the wider context of the experiences of hidden children during the Holocaust, Claire and Ollie's reunion with their parents is extraordinary. That Nel had the foresight to keep the Friedbergs alive in the girls' minds is a testament to her strength; that she willingly

10 Wolf, 113.

returned them to their parents is a testament to her moral fibre. For Rudolph and Sophia Friedberg to welcome Tantel Nel into their family for the rest of their lives speaks to their solidity and their values.

Claire Baum initially wrote *The Hidden Package* because she consciously – even self-consciously – wanted to leave a legacy for her children and grandchildren. This legacy is all the more precious because of the hardship suffered along the way. In leaving behind this cultural inheritance – the story of what it was like to be a hidden child – Claire Baum grounds future generations and helps them understand their origins. This notion of future generations is not just about family, but about humanity. Claire fulfills her goal of teaching readers about the enormity of the Holocaust and the need for cooperation rather than discrimination and thereby leaves a legacy to us all.

Carolyne Van Der Meer
2014

The Netherlands

NORTH
SEA

Westerbork Camp

Zuiderzee

AMSTERDAM
Soestduinen

The Hague
Utrecht

Rotterdam

Rhine

Middelburg

Meuse

Schelde

BELGIUM

Cologne

BRUSSELS

GERMANY

N

0   50   100km

© 2014 - The Azrieli Foundation

In memory of my parents

Rudolph David Friedberg (1908–1978)
A man with great foresight and determination
and
Sophia Aaltjen Friedberg (1909–2009)
Together you saved us and our future generations.

I dedicate this memoir to my parents and to the many very special, courageous people who helped us survive. I never could have written this memoir without all the information they provided me.

To the Duchene family for risking their lives and rescuing us.

To the Canadian army for liberating us.

To Tante Nel: there are not enough words to describe her care and exceptional courage to save us. How lucky we were – our Tante Nel was a very special lady.

To Mrs. Heijkoop for her perseverance in locating us. Though it took many years, with the help of Amnesty International she was finally able to send us our package, our life story filled with long suppressed memories, left behind in her mother's crawl cellar during World War II.

To my dad, 'Pap', for his determination to find hiding places for all of us. Sadly, my dad was not able to celebrate his oldest granddaughter's wedding – he would have been so proud! Unfortunately, his time was too short to experience the joy his family could have given him. He now would have been the proud grandfather of five grandchildren and nine great-grandchildren.

To my mother, 'Mam', for her encouragement always. She was blessed with a long life in good health and was fortunate to have celebrated her ninety-ninth birthday with her children, grandchildren and great-grandchildren and to have seen her wonderful family grow up. We were all blessed with her presence, wisdom and great sense of humour.

To both my parents, Mam and Pap, for making the ultimate sacrifice to give us to total strangers in order to save us. Also, because of their decision to leave Holland, it was here in Canada that I met my dear husband and was able to raise my children and grandchildren in freedom. They left us a true legacy.

To Seymour, my husband, for his patience, help and support.

Author's Preface

A letter from a stranger, who enclosed a package of letters, photographs and drawings from when I was a child during 1942–1945, a time totally forgotten, opened up an entire chapter of my life. For more than twenty-five years, it inspired me to speak to students about this very difficult and dangerous time in history. My focus has been to educate young people on either an elementary, high school or university level to make them understand the enormity of the Holocaust and to teach them cooperation rather than discrimination.

After I spoke, I was always asked, "Why have you not written a book?" Since my parents, in their modesty, had never felt that our story was anything special, I decided, about four years ago, to write a memoir about our hiding and survival to leave as a legacy for my children and grandchildren. But now, in tribute to my parents, who have since passed away, and with the help of the Azrieli Foundation, our story will be told not only to my family but also to all those who are curious to find out what it was like to be a hidden child during World War II.

"Discrimination and hate destroys our foundation. Understanding and cooperation are the building blocks for a safe foundation."

Claire Baum
2013

May 23, 1993

Dear Tante Nel:

As the train tracks clatter beneath me, I think of the helpless ones who heard this sound, but as I hear it again, I am also reminded of those days fifty years ago when I heard the same clatter of the train tracks on our way to you – your home – and today I still wonder and ask, "Why did you do it?" The answer for you was very simply, "I had no choice. How could I let two small children die? There was no other way!"

Again, as I look at you today, I see a strong, unassuming, caring individual. You are a rock, immovable with strong beliefs and convictions, and therefore you almost appear unemotional but on the contrary, your emotions ran and still run very deep and full of love.

Life has not treated you kindly, as you always were the caregiver to your entire family: your parents, brothers, children and grandchildren.

It is fitting that today is Hemelvaartsdag. It was on this day that according to the Christian religion Christ rose to heaven. I believe you are the angel God sent down to earth from heaven.

Soon you will be eighty years old and are in relatively good health. I hope to be able to visit with you for many more years to come.

Forever grateful,
Clary

Our Forgotten Past

On February 21, 1984, one of the coldest days of the winter, we were busy making our final arrangements for the wedding of our eldest daughter, Dianne. With the wedding merely ten days away, Dianne was having the final fitting of her dress. She would be wearing my gown, the wedding dress I had worn on October 28, 1956. The beginning of a wonderful life.

When my mother saw how beautiful and radiant her granddaughter looked in her daughter's gown, her memory went back to her own wedding. The date was July 26, 1934. At the time, many people, including Mam's parents and Pap's business associate, had advised them not to marry – it was during the Depression, just after Hitler had been appointed chancellor of Germany, and the world situation seemed rather ominous and dangerous. She thought back to the life she had lived in luxury, only to be interrupted when her parents, my grandparents, were taken away in the prime of their lives. And of course she missed her husband, my dad, who had passed away several years prior to the wedding. He would have been so proud to see his oldest grandchild get married.

Dianne's wedding was March 3, so I decided to go to the mailbox and check for replies. To my amazement, among the replies I found a letter addressed to me from a stranger, a Mrs. Heijkoop from Rotterdam, Holland, dated February 10, 1984. I didn't recognize the name and asked Mam if she did. She said the name Heijkoop was not familiar to her and asked why now, forty years after World War II, should I receive a letter from a stranger in Holland? Mam insisted that she did not know this person; I figured that the past was so deeply buried in her mind, a time in her life she wanted to forget. Perhaps she was also trying to protect me from our painful past.

Although Mam did not want me to open the letter, I nevertheless felt I had to – there had to be a reason why it had been sent to me. Mrs. Heijkoop was simply asking if I could identify myself, as it had taken her so many years to find out if a package found in her mother's cellar belonged to our family.

I was baffled – how had she found me? I also wondered why a package belonging to our family was hidden in her mother's home. I wanted to speak to her immediately but I could not; it worried me that Mam was so skeptical, so I decided to think it over and to call her in a few days. When I finally phoned, I spoke to a wonderful, caring person who was delighted to have found me after all these years. She relayed how, after her mother passed away, she was cleaning out her basement and, to her surprise, came across a small package in the crawl cellar. When she opened it, she found letters, drawings and photographs of two little girls. She vaguely recalled that a Jewish couple was hiding in her mother's home for a short while during World War II and supposed that in their hurry, they had left this package behind.

Mrs. Heijkoop had been determined to find the package's rightful owner. She hadn't been able to find any record as to where we lived, so she assumed that we left Holland after the war, but she had no idea where we had gone. She contacted the Netherlands' immigration department; however, all they could tell her was that in 1948 our family had been issued passports to an unspecified destination. The only further information they were able to provide her with was that we were not issued an immigration visa and had left Holland in 1951 with a visitor's permit.

After she had exhausted all her sources, she contacted Amnesty International, who thankfully were able to tell her that we were living somewhere in Canada. She then contacted the Canadian government and discovered that we had become Canadian citizens in 1956, the same year that Seymour and I were married. It was then that she finally had a means to contact our family under my married name: Clara Baum-Friedberg.

As I spoke to Mrs. Heijkoop, I knew she was a very special person to have been so committed to finding us. I was totally overcome with emotion as, gradually, some of my suppressed memories started coming back. I remembered the time that my sister and I could not go to school and that Tante Nel had taught us to read and write. I also remembered how she insisted that we write to Mam and Pap, our parents, to keep in touch with them. Then I knew that these had to be our letters, the ones my sister and I wrote while we were in hiding in Soestduinen, our first hiding place, and at Tante Nel's house. I now could understand why Tante Nel insisted we write to our parents – it was their only contact with us. How fortunate we did what she had told us to.

I could only stretch my memory so far and I was curious as to what other memories would come back on seeing the letters we had written as children. On March 1, 1984, our package arrived. Was it an omen for it to come just then, two days before the wedding? Even though it was addressed to me, it did not only belong to me. It belonged to Mam and Pap, as well as to both Ollie and me. I asked my sister, Ollie, if she wanted to open it. She said that she would rather not. She did not seem interested in looking at it. I believe that she didn't want to be reminded of those years, since she was too young and remembered very little.

When I opened the parcel, I was confronted with the past, memories long forgotten. The pictures, letters, photographs and drawings described happy as well as sad moments while Ollie and I were in hiding and separated from Mam and Pap. This package was our diary from 1942 to 1945.

Our parents had never spoken about the past and Mam did not

want to be reminded again. She told me that Pap had made all their decisions, so I had to find out how my dad arranged for a hiding place for himself and for my mother, and how he found a separate address for Ollie and me. Why did he split our family up and decide to give us, his only two little girls, to total strangers? What a courageous thing to do in order to save our lives.

To search for information about those dangerous years, I went to my father's desk, which was given to me and hadn't been emptied after he passed away. To my surprise, in the bottom drawer, I found a file marked "The War Years." I was curious that he had this file tucked away. Was it left there for me? As I rummaged through it, I grew increasingly amazed that he had saved so many documents. I found a visa application form, dated 1939, for our family to immigrate to the United States, which was subsequently refused. I also came across a letter stating that he had joined the Dutch Resistance, his employment record, which stopped in 1942, the exact date we went into hiding, as well as many other papers.[1]

With my dad's information, along with the contents of the package from Mrs. Heijkoop, I was finally able to fill in the missing pieces to write about our hiding and survival during World War II. Although this was a memory I wanted to forget, I felt I should not, because Ollie and I, as only innocent children, were not the heroes in our story. Our story needed to be told because we owed our lives to the many heroes – our parents, the Resistance, the Duchene family, the Canadian army, and a very special lady we fondly called Tante Nel, our caregiver, our war mother. They all were real heroes.

Our story is therefore not only about how we survived but, rather, why we survived.

---

[1]   For information on the Dutch Resistance, as well as on other major organizations; historical, religious and cultural terms; significant historical events and people; geographical locations; and foreign-language words and expressions contained in the text, please see the glossary.

The New Rules

It is difficult to write about what it felt like, not being with our parents for so many years. Our life was certainly far from normal. Although we did not suffer any physical pain, having to hide throughout three years of our childhood was emotionally painful and lonely. I was born in January 1936, and my sister, Olga, was born in December 1937, in Rotterdam. She was only two, and I four, at the outbreak of the war in the Netherlands.

Ever since Hitler had been appointed chancellor of Germany in 1933, he was wielding more power daily and his Nazi Party was receiving overwhelming support. My dad became very aware of how the Jewish people were being targeted in Germany, which became even more evident in 1938 during Kristallnacht, a pogrom that saw thousands of Jewish people arrested, some murdered, their businesses vandalized and Jewish books and manuscripts destroyed or burned.

With Holland's borders touching Germany's, we were practically next-door neighbours, and my dad felt it would not take too long before the Dutch-Jewish population would also be victimized. Therefore, in February 1939, my dad gathered all the necessary documentation – birth certificates, inoculation certificates – in order to apply for visas to immigrate to the United States, not only for our immediate family but for both sets of our grandparents as well.

My paternal grandfather, Jossel, had a very responsible position with the Harbour Commission in Rotterdam and Mam's parents, Jacob and Clara, owned a large wallpaper factory in Rotterdam. In all their business dealings with Germany they had never experienced any anti-Jewish sentiments and neither could see the urgency to leave Holland and everything behind. My dad, however, saw that there were storm clouds on the horizon and that he had to make a crucial decision for the four of us. Instinctively, he felt that it was time for us to leave. Unfortunately, the American government refused our visa, informing us that the immigration quota had been filled. We were doomed to stay behind and face the uncertainties.

On May 10, 1940, shortly after our visa was denied, German paratroopers landed in Holland. The occupation was swift. Within a few days, the German air force, the Luftwaffe, bombed Rotterdam, our birthplace. The centre of our city was totally destroyed, more than nine hundred people were killed and many were injured. Meanwhile, heavy fighting took place near Arnhem, about a hundred kilometres away, and by May 15 we were under German occupation. We were at war! My dad's intuition had been correct.

The German leadership, headed by Seyss-Inquart – a Nazi official – immediately took over. Our queen was forced to leave. She and her government fled to England and Princess Juliana took up residency in Canada. From that time on we were in trouble, although at first, we still lived a rather normal life. We had our own home and were surrounded by our friends, parents and grandparents, whom I have wonderful memories of. They were so proud of Ollie and me and visiting them was always very special. When we listened to their gramophone, my grandmother would insist we take turns sitting on her lap. We knew they loved us so very much.

We also enjoyed visiting our aunts and uncles, Aunt Rosa and Uncle Joe, and Aunt Leni and Uncle Ies, my mother's brothers and sisters-in-law. Aunt Rosa was very pretty and I remember that Ollie and I were all dressed up for her and Uncle Joe's wedding. Sometimes we visited Oom (Uncle) Ari, but we never wanted to because we were both afraid of him. With his great big moustache, he was scary-looking, and he also insisted we kiss him hello and goodbye. However, we were taught to never argue with Mam and Pap, so we had no choice, even though Ollie used to cry every time. I used to tell Ollie to play with the fringes on his carpet and be quiet until we could sneak out without him noticing.

One Sunday, Mam and Pap drove us to the village of Volendam, where everyone wore complete Dutch costumes with lace bonnets and wooden shoes. We asked Mam if we, too, could wear one for a day and have our picture taken. Mam agreed and surprised us by changing her dress as well so the three of us could be in a photo together.

Although we tried to live a normal life, we certainly knew we were at war. There were nightly blackouts during which our windows had to be covered up with black paper. We were afraid of another bombing and we slept with our shoes and bags beside us in case we had to run away.

Gradually, changes were taking place. When I asked if we could visit Aunt Rosa and Uncle Joe again, I was told that they were not at home, that they had gone on a trip somewhere. Mam didn't want to tell me that, fearing for their safety, they had left Holland. I didn't ask about Uncle Ari; I didn't care and was hoping that he had left as well. My parents, though, knew that he had been arrested and it was no longer possible to visit him.

Our life was in turmoil. When my dad's concern for our family's safety grew, he decided to join the underground resistance movement. He joined along with a gentile friend, Pauw. By working together for the Resistance, they were privy to a great deal of information and came to know very well that the Jewish people would be targeted by Holland's own Nazi Party, the National Socialist Movement (NSB), which had a very large membership.

Throughout the next year, the Nazis implemented many new rules, which everyone in the Netherlands had to obey. In the summer of 1941, we had to hand in our radios, our only communication with the rest of the world. Under occupation, we weren't able to find out anything about the war and being forbidden to possess a radio left us isolated. Fortunately, the Resistance kept in touch with English broadcasts by listening to their illegal radios in their basements. My dad spoke and understood German and was able to find out even more by following German broadcasts as well.

By January 1942, every citizen was given strict orders to carry an identification card and Jewish people were identified with the letter J beside their names. Because we had a particularly Jewish-sounding name, Friedberg, my dad contacted a branch of the Resistance to falsify my parents' identification cards. These falsified cards were almost identical to the originals, with two exceptions: they each showed a false name and, most importantly, the letter J did not appear. In the event they were questioned, they could never be identified as being Jewish.

As more rules were implemented, our life became extremely difficult, nearly intolerable. In April, Jews six years and older had to wear the yellow Star of David. We could only shop between certain hours. Jewish professionals – doctors, lawyers, teachers – could no longer practise. Jewish stores had to close. We could not go to school. That summer, we had to hand in all our personal belongings, including our bicycles. Every day, we could expect even more rules and if we did not abide by them, we would be arrested.

Some people didn't hand in all their belongings, particularly their bicycles, their only mode of transportation. One of our Jewish neighbours had bought a new bike and decided not to hand it over. He tried to fool the Nazis by turning in his old bicycle instead. Someone must have reported him. The next morning the entire family was arrested and thrown onto a truck, along with their new bicycle, and were never heard from again.

Soon, all men in the Netherlands would be drafted to work in a German forced labour camp but at first many men, including my maternal grandfather, Jacob, volunteered. He trusted the German people because he did so much business with Germany, and he was not afraid to work hard. He volunteered his services, believing, as they'd been told, they'd be sent to a labour camp in Germany. He went to Building 24, located at the harbour near the railway station, which served as the first gathering place for the Jews of Rotterdam and the southern provinces of the Netherlands.

At the time, no one was aware that he, as well as the other Jewish men there, would actually be sent to a place called Westerbork, located in one of Holland's northern provinces on the German border. It was a transit camp, a gathering place from where, not long after arrival, Jews were sent to the Nazi death camps or concentration camps of Auschwitz, Sobibor, Theresienstadt or Bergen-Belsen. Sadly, very few returned.

By July 1942, Jewish men were forcefully rounded up. From then until October 1942, the roundups really accelerated. My dad, with the help of the Resistance, was hopeful he could still find a safe home, a hiding place for our family as well as for some of his friends. He begged my grandmother Clara to go into hiding, telling her it would be easier to hide her alone, since Grandfather had already volunteered to work in Germany. But she, as well as all the others he tried to convince, refused his offer. Even the Aarons family, one of Pap's closest friends, couldn't see the urgency of going into hiding. They all believed they would survive and thought that my dad was being the ultimate pessimist.

That October, Jews were systematically arrested and deported. An alphabetical list of Jewish names and addresses, from a census published by the Dutch government the year before, was posted at our City Hall in Rotterdam. This census had been requested by the Nazis, and made it very convenient for them to arrest all Jews who lived in Rotterdam.

Arrests were being made in alphabetical order and my parents grew concerned when they were unable to get in touch with the Aarons. They wondered what had happened to their friends and worried whether they had been arrested – their name had to have been one of the first on the list. If only they would have listened to my dad when he so desperately tried to convince the three of them to go into hiding....

Two weeks later, on a Friday evening, my grandmother came to our house for Shabbat dinner. I didn't know why my grandfather wasn't with her; they were always together, particularly on Shabbat, and my mother told me only that he was very busy with work. As soon as my grandmother finished her dinner, she was very anxious to get home, wanting to obey the curfew and be home before dark. She quickly said her goodbyes and left. She was in so much of a hurry that my parents never had a chance to really say goodbye to her. Unfortunately, this was to be her final goodbye.

When my grandmother arrived home, either the SS or the Dutch police must have been waiting for her. We later heard that her house was raided and she was arrested. She had received several letters from my grandfather while he was at Westerbork and she must have assumed that she, too, was being taken there, hoping to be reunited with my grandfather.

After that night, we lost all contact with her. My parents' only hope was that she was with my grandfather. We knew how anxious she was to see him again. We never received any letters from either of them and never found out if they were reunited. It wasn't until after the war that we learned that both were deported to Auschwitz and most likely never saw each other at Westerbork.

Because we lived around the corner from our grandparents, whose last name was Cohen, it was logical that we, the Friedbergs, were going to be the next victims. My dad was extremely concerned and immediately got in touch with the Resistance. He spoke to his friend Pauw, hoping the Resistance could find a hiding place for the two of us, as well as for Mam and himself; he had decided to split the family up, knowing it would have been too dangerous for us all to hide together. My father's first priority was to secure a hiding place for Ollie and me. We were lucky. My father's friend Pauw did not disappoint him – he had found a family who were prepared to take us into their home. It was more difficult for the Resistance to find a family willing to take the chance of hiding my parents. Many were too afraid, but after a series of refusals, they succeeded.

Separation

One afternoon, while I was looking for one of my dolls to play with, I overheard Mam and Pap discussing something about another home for us. I didn't quite understand why, but since they were talking for a very long time, I thought it had to be important.

Before I went to bed, Mam and Pap told me that Ollie and I were to go away with someone named Pauw the next day. They wanted to wait until the morning to mention it to Ollie. I asked who Pauw was, as I hadn't met him, but I didn't question why we would be going away. I understood that Mam and Pap must have had a very good reason. I thought about what they had said to each other in the afternoon, even though I was not supposed to be listening.

Ever since the outbreak of the war, the Germans had installed rockets in the park next to our house. These rockets were fired from various locations in Europe and, in Holland, from Rotterdam. At night, when the rockets were sent, the noise was deafening. Lying in bed, I couldn't help hearing that horrible screeching sound. I had been getting somewhat used to it, however, that particular night, they sounded louder than ever. I plugged my ears, but it didn't help. Every time they flew over our house it was scary enough, but I was even more worried as to what I was going to face the next day. How was I going to tell Ollie that we had to leave Mam and Pap?

Every morning, Mam and Pap would wake us up at 7:00 a.m. On

that particular morning in October, their greeting seemed different. They appeared nervous while we had our breakfast, and they were whispering to each other. When we finished eating, they asked us to listen very carefully. Then they told us that we, Ollie and me, were going away for a little while. Although it wasn't a surprise to me, I was still afraid because I didn't know where, and for how long, we would be gone.

My sister, being two years younger than me, thought that she was going on a holiday with Mam and Pap. She packed her little suitcase and was excited to go away. Ollie didn't understand that our parents were sending the two of us away without them. I, however, understood very well that we were not going on a holiday.

Before we left, we were given strict instructions never to talk to strangers. We were to act as nieces of our new family and we would be brought up as Christians. We were to tell anyone who asked that Mam was in the hospital and that Pap was working in Germany. It was a very believable alibi, a fabrication we would be forced to tell in order to survive. No one was ever to know that we were Jewish.

A little later, a stranger whom we were told to call Oom Pauw came to pick us up. I still didn't ask our parents why we had to go; I knew we had to. We both kissed Mam and Pap goodbye and went with Oom Pauw, the Resistance worker, to the train station in Rotterdam where we boarded a train. Our destination was Soestduinen, less than a hundred kilometres away but, to me, far away from Rotterdam, our home.

I can still remember how Oom Pauw lifted us up into the train because the step was much too high. I also recall that we had to transfer and I believe it was in Amersfoort where we waited inside the station for our connection. Meanwhile, Oom Pauw gave us something to eat. While we were eating our sandwiches, through the window we saw soldiers marching up and down the platform. Oom Pauw didn't want to draw attention to us and he told us not to be afraid and not to look at anyone, just to pay attention to our food.

We didn't know where exactly Oom Pauw was taking us but after an hour's train ride we arrived at our new home in Soestduinen, "the sand dunes of Soest." This little village on the coast of the North Sea was located near the queen's summer palace in Soest. Her palace either stood empty or was occupied by the Nazis when our queen was forced to leave Holland in 1940 at the outbreak of the war. We were far away from Rotterdam, far away from Mam and Pap.

We didn't know what to expect. We didn't know our new family, the Duchenes. We were told to call the lady Tante (Aunt) Kor and her husband Oom Piet and we were given strict instructions to be polite. When we arrived, Tante Kor and Oom Piet came to the door. We knew we had to say hello but we were both so nervous and shy that we hesitated for a few minutes before either of us could speak.

Tante Kor realized we were nervous and tried to make us feel at home. She took Ollie's suitcase and asked both of us if we wanted to see our bedroom. The bedroom was an attic room just large enough for two beds, one for each of us. Then she showed us the rest of the house, which was a real country home. When she took us outside, we could see a forest. Tante Kor told us that we could walk into the forest by following the path beside their house, which also led directly to the sand dunes.

Mam and Pap had mentioned that Tante Kor and Oom Piet had a daughter named Jopie, who was a little older than we were. We were anxious to meet her and wondered where she was. Tante Kor said that she was at school and would be back momentarily. When Jopie came home we were so happy because we now had a friend to spend time with.

Ollie and I took some time to get used to living with Tante Kor and Oom Piet. It was very different from living in Rotterdam, where we were surrounded by family. Now, we were surrounded by strangers. Although they did their best to make us welcome, it was not the same as being with Mam and Pap.

Before Jopie went to school we had breakfast with her. Afterward,

Tante Kor let us play in the breakfast room. At our new home in the country, there were all kinds of mice running around but we had to get used to it. We discovered mouse droppings everywhere. We had to stay at home during school hours and Tante Kor kept us busy during the day by teaching us how to sew and knit and how to mend the holes in our socks. We were glad we were being cared for and that Jopie was our new friend. Oom Piet and Tante Kor were so patient and kind that Ollie and I never felt that we were treated differently from their own daughter.

A bedroom in our new home. By Claire Baum, age six.

On December 4, 1942, we were busy preparing for the next day, St. Nikolaas Day, when Sinterklaas and his helper, Zwarte Piet, would come all the way from Spain to our house to bring us presents. In preparation for their arrival, Tante Kor had told us to leave our wooden shoes, *klompen*, filled with straw and a bowl of water beside the fireplace in case Sinterklaas' horse was thirsty after their long trip. We could hardly wait for tomorrow.

On December 5, when we woke up, we wondered why Oom Piet was not down for breakfast. When we asked Tante Kor, she said that he had gone to work but he never worked on Saturdays so we didn't really believe her. We also didn't believe in Sinterklaas and figured that Oom Piet was getting dressed up as Sinterklaas and that Jopie would be dressed as Zwarte Piet. We had to pretend to believe in him, though, or we wouldn't get any presents.

That same evening, Sinterklaas and Zwarte Piet arrived at our house. Oom Piet and Jopie were not at home and we knew why. Sinterklaas asked if we had been good girls because if we had, he had presents for us. Then Zwarte Piet opened his bag, which was filled with presents. He handed Tante Kor a note to give to Ollie. It read: "Ollie, Sinterklaas knows it will be your birthday on December 7. Because you have been such a good girl, on your birthday you will receive a big surprise." Fortunately Ollie didn't have to wait too long to find out, since it was only two days away.

December 7, Ollie's birthday, was a wonderful day; everyone wanted to celebrate with her. Jopie walked in with Peter, our neighbour, and our other friends came too, all carrying presents under their arms. Ollie was excited to open them but before she did, she showed our friends what Sinterklaas had brought for us.

Then Tante Kor carried in a birthday cake she had baked. On it there were six candles because Ollie was five years old and there was one for good luck. Ollie was asked to cover her eyes and blow the candles out while she made a secret wish. When she opened her eyes, she was so surprised to see that her wish had come true! Tante Kor carried in her surprise, a doll carriage with a beautifully outfitted doll inside.

We were Christians now, and were getting ready to celebrate Christmas and New Year's with the Duchene family. Oom Piet, who worked at a lamp factory, asked Tante Kor to make costumes in the shape of light bulbs for an upcoming Christmas play. Tante Kor was handy and knew how to sew but because she had to have them ready in two weeks, she asked us to help her. She had taught us how to sew and knit and we were happy to help. We had to string chicken wire in the shape of a light bulb to make a skirt, which Tante Kor then covered with white material. To complete the costumes, she made a gold-coloured hat to resemble the top of the bulb. When she finished, we were amazed to see that these skirts really did look like light bulbs.

We soon guessed that the actors were to be dressed up as Christmas lights and lamps. Oom Piet told us the play was called "A Living Christmas Tree" and that all the actors would be wearing our costumes. We asked Tante Kor if we could go to see the play, but she told us that it was strictly for the employees. Although I was disappointed, I understood why they couldn't take us. It would be too dangerous.

Tante Kor had been so busy with the play that she had forgotten to make a Christmas house, which was an annual tradition. She hurried to make one out of a cardboard box and she had us help her by cutting out twelve windows and covering them with red crepe paper, which represented the twelve days leading up to Christmas. For twelve nights, we opened one window until Christmas Day.

On December 25, Christmas morning, all the windows of our Christmas house were open. Ollie and I had never seen a Christmas tree. When we came downstairs for breakfast we couldn't believe our eyes! There, in the middle of the living room, stood a tree completely decorated with angels, little bells in various colours, and lots of candies. We could not get over how beautiful it looked and could only imagine that it must have taken Tante Kor and Oom Piet a long time to decorate the tree; they must have been very busy while we were sleeping.

One month later, on January 25, 1943, I had a wonderful celebration for my seventh birthday. Tante Kor baked a cake with eight candles on it – seven plus one for good luck. Tante Kor gave me a bathing suit and our best friend, Peter, gave me a skipping rope. When I was asked to make a wish, I did not wish for presents; I had received them already. My secret wish was to see Mam and Pap. Before I went to bed, I asked Tante Kor for a postcard to write on and I also wrote a letter to Mam and Pap. I wanted to tell them about my special day.

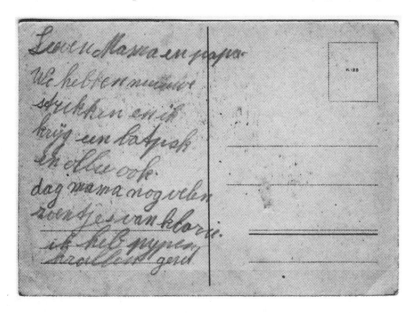

Dear Mama and Papa:
We have new bows in our hair. Ollie and I are getting a bathing suit.
Many kisses, Clary

⌣

We had stayed indoors most of the winter and by March we were thrilled that it was finally springtime and that we could go outside. Our biggest thrill was to go to the sand dunes on the weekend when Jopie didn't go to school and Peter could come with us as well. We had the best time making sandcastles and playing all kinds of games. One time, I brought along the bathing suit that Tante Kor had given me for my birthday. I was hoping to go swimming in the sea, but the water was still too chilly. I would have to wait until summer.

The following Saturday, when we wanted to play in the sand and climb on the dunes again, Tante Kor said that only she and Jopie could go with us because Peter had told her that he had too much homework to do. We were disappointed, having always had so much fun with him.

When we came home, I noticed Tante Kor picked something up from her doorstep. I thought that it looked like the yellow Star of David. I was scared. Had it been left there for me? I knew I was supposed to have worn it when I turned six years old but of course Mam and Pap would never have given it to me then; and of course would never have let me wear it. Tante Kor thought about who could have left it on her doorstep. One of her neighbours? Peter's father, who was a member of the NSB Party? She knew that it was for me to wear – Ollie was too young.

When I went to bed, Tante Kor showed it to me. She told me not to worry and that I did not have to wear it. She emphasized that I was "a Christian now" and Christian people didn't have to wear the yellow star. The Nazis had made a mistake, she said, she was going to throw it out. Before she did, she asked Oom Piet what he thought she should do. He insisted that she destroy the evidence. She threw it in the fireplace and burned it. We were happy; we were safe, for now. No one would find out anything about us!

We thought that Peter, who lived next door, was our friend, although he always asked too many questions. It turned out that he didn't believe that we were nieces of the Duchenes and his suspicions must have led him to assume that we were Jewish. Peter belonged to the Nazi Party for young boys, called the Nationale Jeugdstorm, and was anxious to betray us so that he would be considered a hero by the Party. He had approached his dad about his suspicions.

We were lucky that Peter's dad felt sorry not only for us, but also for the Duchene family. He realized that all of our lives were in danger and knew that we would be arrested by one of his NSB Party friends. First, he scolded his son and told him that he was wrong, we were family, and to forget it at once. He knew very well, however, that his son was not wrong.

That very night, he went to see Tante Kor and Oom Piet and begged them to take us away immediately. He felt that it was his duty to warn his neighbour. When it got dark, Tante Kor and Oom Piet took us on their bikes back to the train station where Oom Pauw, our Resistance worker, was waiting for us.

We were lucky – we had escaped!

To A Different Home

In the spring of 1943, it was extremely difficult and dangerous to find us another home to hide in. Most Jewish people were either already hiding in Christian homes or had been sent to a concentration camp. Oom Pauw didn't know where he could take us. Out of desperation, he thought of his sister, Nel. She was twenty-eight years old, her husband was working in Germany, and she had no children, so he was hoping she could look after us for a few days until he could find us another place. When he asked her, she did not hesitate, saying, "Of course, I don't have a choice; how could I let these two little children die?"

Oom Pauw told us that Nel was looking forward to meeting us and was very happy to have us stay with her. We were back on the train, going back to our birthplace of Rotterdam, but to another home. Although Oom Pauw told us not to be afraid and that we'd be staying with his sister, we didn't know what to expect. When we arrived, we were greeted by a very pretty lady whom we were to call Tante Nel. In a way, she resembled Mam, which was strange because now she was going to be our new mother/caregiver. She welcomed us with such warmth that our fears dissolved.

Tante Nel lived in a basement apartment. She led us into the front room of her three-room apartment, the living room, where we saw two mattresses on the floor, one for me to sleep on and one for Ollie.

That first night while we were supposed to be sleeping, I was awake all night from the sound of the clock on the mantle, which chimed every hour. I wondered if this room was to be our permanent bedroom and secretly hoped that we did not have to sleep on the floor in this room forever.

After a few days, Tante Nel gave us the middle room. She realized that it was difficult for us to sleep on her living room floor. Jan, Tante Nel's youngest brother, had cleared out the furniture in the middle room, which was just large enough for a double bed. However, there stood only a single bed for Ollie and me to share. We couldn't lie side by side. We had to sleep head to foot together in this little bed.

In Soestduinen, before we came to Tante Nel, we each had a single bed, so to share one was very different. We weren't used to it, but we didn't care. We knew we were going to be happy with Tante Nel. At first, Oom Pauw said that we could only stay at Tante Nel's for a few days but she was such a very special, kind lady that we were hoping we could stay longer – we didn't want to leave again. The way she looked after us, it was hard for us to believe that she had no children.

Oom Pauw tried once more to find us somewhere else to hide, but it was impossible. It was 1943 – no one was willing to take us in. We had to stay with Tante Nel. Although she could never have replaced our real parents, Mam and Pap, we didn't mind living with her. When her brother told her that he was not able to find us another home, Tante Nel let us stay in the middle room. It became our bedroom with a double bed to share. She knew that we would not be able to sleep head to foot in such a little bed forever.

It was the beginning of April when we arrived at Tante Nel's home and since April 7 was Pap's birthday, Tante Nel asked us to make him a birthday card. We were surprised that Tante knew it was Pap's birthday. She showed us that on her bathroom wall hung a birthday calendar with everyone's birthdays on it, even Mam and Pap's. To Tante Nel, birthdays were always very important and very special. Even after the war, none of our birthdays were ever forgotten.

When I asked Ollie if she could make Pap a birthday card and colour it in while I wrote the birthday greeting, she insisted that she write to Pap also. Tante Nel knew that it would make Mam and Pap very happy. We promised Tante Nel that we would always write to Mam and Pap, even if it was not for a birthday.

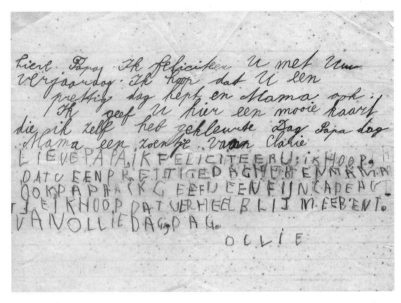

April 7, 1943
Dear Papa:
I wish you a Happy Birthday. I hope you and Mama will have a nice day. Ollie made a nice birthday card. I helped her colour it. She will try to write to you also. I am wishing you a Happy Birthday. Bye, and a kiss from, Clary.
Dear Papa:
I wish you a happy day. I give you a nice present a card and hope you will be happy with it. Bye, bye, Ollie.

∽

Once our letters were written, they were given to Oom Pauw, Tante Nel's brother, to deliver to our parents. He knew where they were hiding; he was the only stranger we could trust. Tante Nel couldn't know where my parents were and my parents didn't know where we were, should either one of us be questioned by a collaborator, or worse, arrested. During the war you couldn't trust anyone, not even your best friend, the corner grocery store clerk or your neighbour. Holland had many collaborators.

When Oom Pauw came back with letters from Mam and Pap, we opened them right away. The letters made our day very special. We were so lucky that Mam and Pap were able to stay in touch with us.

We soon came to call Tante Nel's parents, the Wielaards, Oma and Opa (Grandma and Grandpa). They lived next door, in the back of their glass store; from the street, no one could tell that there were living quarters behind the store. The Wielaards supplied and installed glass windows, and we were never allowed to go into their store. They told us that they were worried we would cut ourselves on the glass, but I also think that they were afraid we could be seen and purposely kept us in the back. Whenever we went to Oma and Opa Wielaard's house, we had to enter through their back door.

The Wielaards had three sons, Pauw, Leen and Jan. Jan lived with Oma and Opa Wielaard and worked for them as well. His job was to cut the panes of glass to size in his workshop, which was in their basement. Pauw and Leen lived around the corner and visited often.

We spent time and ate most of our meals with Tante Nel's parents, who were devout Christians. When we sat down to eat, we had to say grace before and after each meal. When we were finished eating, before we were allowed to get up from the table, Oma Wielaard would tell us to pay attention as she read us a different chapter of the Bible. We knew to pay attention; when she had finished reading, she would ask us questions. She was very strict.

When we were finally allowed to get up from the table, we could go into their backyard chicken coop, where Oma and Opa kept chickens and roosters that woke us up every morning. Once a day we fed them grain and looked for eggs, even though Oma said that her chickens had to be at least six months old before laying eggs. She was emphatic that it wasn't the right time so when we went into the chicken coop, we were astonished to find eggs. When we told Oma, she at first said that it was impossible but, being a Christian, she believed it to be a miracle.

Dear Papa and Mama:
I liked the paper doll. I have already cut it out. Tante bought chicks. They are already eight weeks old. Tante has said that once they are six months old they will lay eggs. Once in a while we get an egg to eat. We

also have had tomatoes. Sometimes Tante bakes bread and makes pan-
cakes. I really like it with sugar. Tante bought three rabbits.

Bye, Papa and Mama, many kisses from Ollie.

～

We were so fond of our pet rabbits, whose cages were in Oma's yard. My rabbit was black and white and Ollie's rabbit was brown. We loved petting them and feeding them celery sticks. They were always hungry.

Because Tante Nel had no children, there were no toys for us to play with. We had to improvise by using our imagination. Sometimes our imagination was so vivid that we really believed what was happening within our surroundings. We even thought that we had a parrot and a dog.

October 7, 1943

Dear Mama and Papa:

We have a dog. He is sitting beside me while I am writing to you. You know, his name is Lulu. Mama, I wish you a happy birthday. We have a parrot. He called us names. At 12:00 we are going roller skating. Mama, listen, there are a lot of people who had to go out of their house. We also had to leave. Many kisses, bye, Clary

～

We weren't allowed to go out during school hours, so our home became our school, where Tante Nel taught us to read and write and Tante Nel's friend Eva taught us arithmetic. They both instructed us to study and to read many books, though we often preferred to play rather than study. Whenever we got a break, we turned to the various craft projects we had on the go. Oma had a spinning wheel and taught us how to use it by guiding the raw sheep's wool through a spindle to make a long strand. Ollie and I took turns. It was quite difficult. After the wool had been spun into a thin thread she showed us how to knit with it. It was very different from cotton, which we were used to, but cotton was so scarce that Tante couldn't get any more, so we had to use the freshly spun wool.

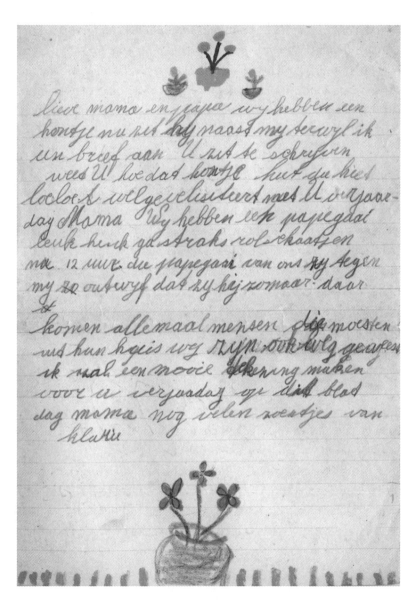

Mama:

I liked the cookies with the sprinkles. We had a nice day. Mama, I have had a haircut. Ollie lost a tooth. We are growing. At our house our leaded windows were damaged but not broken. Mam, my underpants are all worn out. I tried to knit one, but Tante has said we are out of cotton. Mama, Oom Pauw got married and his wife is visiting Oma. Now we cannot go to Oma when she reads from the Bible. We are not studying too much, we really do not want to. Mama, I like the dress, but the coat does not fit Ollie. Mama, I promise to write you back soon. Bye, bye, Clary

~

For another distraction, Tante gave us a cardboard box to play house with. Most of the time I pretended to be Mam and Ollie was Pap, but we took turns. Every night before we went to bed, we imagined we were going on a special trip and we always picked a different destination. At least we had each other and our imagination. The Nazis could never have taken that away from us.

We had to stay indoors until 4:00 p.m. when school ended, and then we were allowed to go outside and play with the neighbourhood children. Our friends in the neighbourhood were curious where we went to school since they never saw us during the day, so we told them that our school was quite far away. We knew we had to pretend that we had been in school, so we carefully listened to what our friends had learned that day and compared our day with theirs. They really believed we had been at another school.

For three years we lived a life of pretense and a constant lie. We realized our lives were in danger and knew we had to lie in order to protect each other, to survive. We knew what hiding meant: to hide our religion; to always be quiet; to never fight or argue with each

uit maar niet stuk.
mama & myn broekjes zyn
haast allemaal versleten
ik heb zelf al een broekje
gebreit maar nu heift tante
geen katoen meer
Mama oom poul is getrouwd
en nu is zyn vrouw
ook by oma Nu kunnen
we niet meer by oma lezen
in de dag Nu blyven we
by tante Maar lezen
doen wy niet nu niet veel
meer want wy hebben niet
veel zin. Nu spelen wy
onder schooltyd lezen willen
wy niet. Mama die jurk
es staan ons netjes Maar
ik heb die blauwe jas en
ol die jas staat ol niet netjes
mama nu heb ik tog wel
uw trug geschreven

other. Our parents were hiding somewhere else and even our toys were hidden. We also knew that we had to find a hiding place in our house or next door, in case our house was searched by the Nazis. These random searches were called *razzias* and it was during one of these searches that we almost lost our lives for the second time.

One day, we were surprised by a lunchtime raid – most house searches took place during the evening. After Oma and Opa's house was searched, Nel knew our turn was going to be next. She told us not to worry and to quietly go to our secret hiding place in the cupboard behind the couch. When Nel looked outside, she couldn't believe that the Nazi soldiers had decided to sit on our doorstep to eat their lunch. They were laughing and joking while they were eating. Ollie and I were so scared. Tante Nel told us to run out the back door to Oma and Opa's house and hide in their backyard. We ran as fast as we could and arrived, trembling. Then, Oma took us into the chicken coop. There was another secret hiding place in Oma and Opa's house, behind the broken glass that was stored in large garbage cans in their basement, but there was no time to hide there; it was safer to stay in the coop. We waited there patiently, hoping they hadn't seen us.

Nel knew that once the soldiers had finished their lunch and stopped laughing, it would have been our turn to have our house searched. Nel stayed at home, unafraid, knowing we were safe with her parents. To Tante Nel's surprise, after their lunch, the soldiers left, moving on to search the next house. They must have forgotten and thought, mistakenly, that our house had already been searched! It was a miracle we had escaped for the second time.

Because we were being brought up as Christians and since the Bible was read to us so many times, often three times a day, we knew this was a miracle. Every night, before we went to sleep, we had to say our prayers and we were told to pray for miracles.

I worried whether Mam and Pap also had a hiding place in case of a house raid. I was hoping that they, too, prayed for miracles. I decided to ask Oom Pauw about both things when he next came to pick our letters up to take them to Mam and Pap. He told me not to worry and explained that Pap had a hiding place in the false ceiling of their house. It was much too dangerous for both Mam and Pap to be together during a search, so Mam would go to a neighbour to hide for a short time in their crawl cellar. Presumably, this was where the package of our letters was later found.

Even though Oom Pauw had told me not to be concerned, I imagined that Mam and Pap must have worried about us all the time and that they must have been anxious to see us again. I had no idea when we would see Mam and Pap again – would they even recognize us? We looked so different with our long hair and pigtails. But in the meantime, we felt very safe with Tante Nel.

I also asked what Mam and Pap did all day. How did they keep busy? They couldn't play imaginary games like us! Oom Pauw told us that Pap was busy making a surprise for us, but that it was too heavy to bring back with him. Pap told Oom Pauw that he would give it to us when he saw us again. I thought about how long it might be until we could see Mam and Pap. What was Pap making for us? I couldn't imagine what it could be; I was sure he could never use a hammer, as it would have made much too much noise.

⁓

Dear Mam and Pap:

I am so happy with the vest you sent me. And the money is in my piggybank. Tante bought ice cream with the money. Mam, you know that sometimes we get an egg. This week we have had two eggs. Tonight we ate tomatoes, cheese and bread. Sometimes I eat seven slices of bread. Tante said that she does not mind if I get fat. With the holidays we played on the street the whole day with our friends. We have new clogs. Kisses, Clary

3

*Mama wy eten ontzettend
veel mama das is waar
dat kosten goed voor ons zo wijs
ik heb afentoe nog wuleens
galbulten maar niet veel
meer*

*Mama ik heb ne
allemaal de groeten van
U gedaan dag mama nog
velen groeten van Cara en
klarie*

Mama: We are eating a lot. Mama, you are right, Tante takes good care of us. Every now and then I get hives. But not too many. Mama, I give regards to all. Bye, Mama.

Regards from Ollie and Clary.

~

On December 7, 1943, we celebrated Ollie's sixth birthday with all our friends. Eva came and we were surprised that Jopie came as well, all the way from Soestduinen. We hadn't seen her for almost a year and had really missed her.

While our friends finished the candies Mam and Pap had sent us, Ollie was busy showing everyone what Sinterklaas had brought on December 5. Then Tante Nel brought in Ollie's birthday cake and she blew the candles out and made her secret wish. I imagined that she was wishing for a new doll since her doll was too big to fit in her carriage.

Ollie and I had had such a good time with our friends on Ollie's birthday, and afterward we were rather sad that we had to stay home all day. Fortunately, Tante Nel thought of something for us to do. She took an old shoe box and we decorated the inside with cotton into a viewing box of a snow scene with children playing. Tante said that we could take it outside at lunchtime or on Saturday and that we could charge the children one penny to take a peek. When Saturday came, our friends couldn't wait to see what we had made.

~

Dear Mama and Papa:

On Ollie's birthday our friends came and ate the candies you gave us and we played with the toys. Sinterklaas brought us cake and now our tummies are full. I received a little chair, a crib for my doll and all kinds of things. Soon it will be Christmas and we will decorate the Christmas tree with balloons, a tote stool and a little plane, a Zeppelin. Mama and Papa, we wish you a healthy new year. Bye Mama and Papa.

With many kisses, from, Clary

Danger Around Us

One day after school, our friends asked us to go for a walk. To our surprise we saw a number of people milling around. We asked them what was happening and were told to go home at once, but we were too curious to listen. All of a sudden, we heard six shots being fired and when we looked around, we saw six men on the ground. We were all frightened, and Ollie and I rushed home to ask Tante the reason we had seen these killings. Tante Nel explained to us that the Nazis had caught these men and killed them for not obeying their rules. It must have been difficult for her to explain that these men were members of the Resistance, just like her own brother Pauw.

It was on May 20, 1944, that we saw Anton Mussert, a Dutch Nazi official. He passed our house on the way to the Coliseum to give another propaganda speech. I knew what he looked like from a picture on a billboard at the corner of the street. I wanted to look out the window to see if he resembled his picture, but Tante Nel soon forbade us and we had to stay behind the curtains. She was afraid we could be spotted in the two-way mirror outside her window. Over the next few days, we were not allowed to be on the street. With Mussert in town, we definitely had to stay indoors. Tante Nel told us that it was a good time to keep busy and write to Mam and Pap.

May 22, 1944
Dear Mama and Papa:
I have a nice present. The rabbit has eleven young ones, they all are big and two are already dead. Mama listen, on May 20 Mussert was in the little N S B house on his way to speak in the Coliseum. Jopie was here

and the chickens have laid eggs. One egg they have eaten themselves – don't you think that was naughty? Janneman had his birthday and received so many presents, too much to mention.

Now I have to stop writing. Bye, many kisses, from Clary

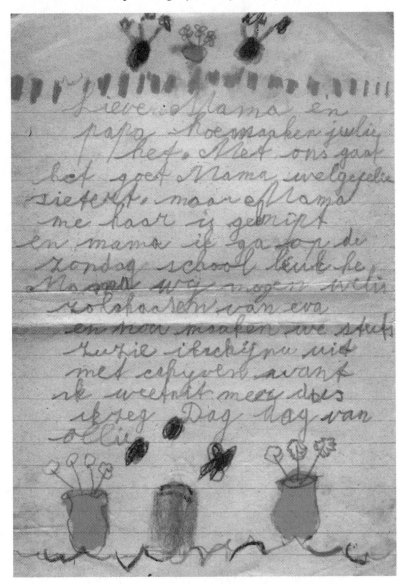

Dear Mama and Papa:

How are you? We are fine. Mama I had a haircut. I have been to Sunday School. Tomorrow we can borrow Eva's roller skates. Now I stop writing. I have nothing else to say. Bye, bye, from Ollie.

~

About a month later, our friends told us that there was going to be a circus in town and asked us if we wanted to go with them to see where the tent was being put up. We were so excited to see the circus tent and talked about what it might be like to go to a real circus. We didn't know if it was possible, but we asked Tante Nel if she could take us; she promised us that she would take us on Saturday when it was a holiday.

When we walked into the circus tent we were greeted by two clowns, who scared us at first but then were so funny that they made us laugh. However, when we looked around I truly got scared. We saw large yellow banners with black lettering all around us. I could read the big black letters that said, "Forbidden for Jews." We had been told to forget that we were Jewish, so we tried not to pay attention to it and to just enjoy the show.

At the opening of the first act we saw lions and tigers doing tricks, which scared us as well. We were hoping that they were well trained so that no one would get hurt. With the lion tamer in the cage, we didn't have to worry. During the second act, we saw a routine with six acrobats, and one lady on a swing all lit up in lights. Ollie and I thought that if we practised, we might be able to do the same tricks. In the third act, horses danced to music. The music was so beautiful that for a little while I forgot we were in a dangerous place.

As we were waiting for the next act to start, Tante Nel told us that it was time for us to go home. At first, we were disappointed; we wanted to stay longer, but we understood that Tante Nel must have had a very good reason. When we came home, Tante Nel made sure that we let Mam and Pap know about our exciting day.

October 10, 1944

Dear Papa and Mama:

Ollie is always eating. At the moment we are doing fine. Once the war is over I will come back to you. The circus was here and it was beautiful. *There were three clowns, they were blowing their trumpets. One of the clowns took his trumpet and placed it on his head. The other clown kept pulling his hair. Don't you think that was funny! Have you ever been to a circus? We would like to go again, but it will not be here much longer. Papa, we are learning and reading many books. This morning, Oma's rooster kept on crowing. That is funny, isn't it? Bye, Clary*

Dear Mama and Papa:
They are taking the circus away, we don't like it.
Bye, many kisses from Olga

The Hunger Winter

During the winter of 1944, hunger was ravaging the country. This period came to be known as the Hunger Winter. Everyone was starving. Food ration cards, only one per family, were distributed; food for one week was meant to last for a month and the rations and food were running out.

By this time, the southern part of Holland had already been liberated, but a part of northern Holland was not. We were isolated from the farms, surrounded by the enemy, and very heavy fighting was taking place at our borders. No food could enter our part of the country because of a railway strike coordinated by the Resistance and the Dutch government-in-exile. The strike was meant to stop the movement of German troops, but, in retaliation, Germany banned food transports. Some people were so hungry that they were even eating out of garbage cans. Community food kitchens would give us only one bowl of soup made out of sugar beets, tulip bulbs and weeds. Hitler was hoping that the entire Dutch population would die of starvation; in fact, nearly 20,000 people did.

We were so hungry that at Christmas time one of our pet rabbits had to be on the table for our Christmas dinner. Before we went to church with Tante Nel to see the Christmas tree, we had to pull straws as to which rabbit had to be chosen for our special dinner.

When we arrived at church we saw how beautifully the Christmas tree was decorated. There were many presents under the tree but we knew there were none for us. When we went home, the table was set. I didn't want to look at it. There on the table was my rabbit, my black-and-white rabbit, to be eaten for our Christmas dinner. Although I was very hungry, I couldn't eat my pet and I was so sad that I cried all night.

It was on my birthday, January 25, 1945, that the Hunger Winter was at its worst. Food rations were scarce and we were very, very hungry. Ollie and I went with Tante Nel to the soup kitchen where we each were again given only one bowl of grey mush, made out of sugar beets and weeds. We had to stand in line for a very long time to get our one bowl and there weren't any second helpings. After we had finished eating, we were still so hungry that our stomachs growled.

I saw many people fainting of hunger while I was waiting in line for our soup. I imagined that some people had died right in front of me. When I asked Tante Nel if they were dying, she pretended not to hear me. I believe she was trying to protect me on my birthday.

Tante Nel told us that one of her neighbours was busy catching seagulls with a fishing hook. He would remove their feathers, cook them, conserve them in jars and sell them. We were hoping that Tante Nel had bought a jar from him and when we came home, she surprised us by showing us a glass jar she had bought. We were excited to open it. Tante Nel said we could have it for dinner since we had only had one bowl of soup to last us the entire day.

After we had been to the soup kitchen, the highlight of the day was to go to a trading bureau, a place where we could bring our old clothes and outgrown shoes and exchange them. When Tante Nel handed in our old shoes, she received someone else's outgrown clothes or shoes. We were so happy, believing we had received a new pair of shoes. We couldn't wait to tell Mam and Pap about our new clothes and shoes.

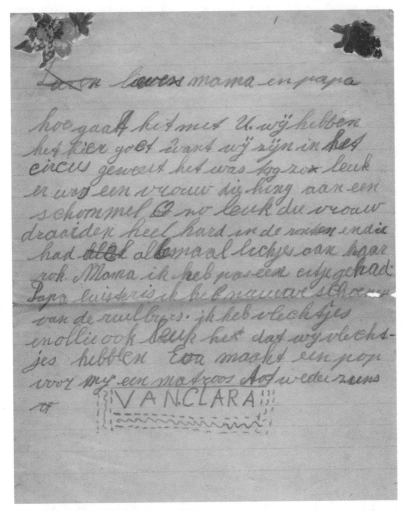

Dear Mama and Papa:

How are you. We are doing well and we have been to the circus. It was so nice. There was a lady hanging from a swing and as she was turning, there were lights on her skirt. Mama, I recently have had a little egg treat. Pap, listen, I have just received new shoes from the Trading Depot. Ollie and I now have pigtails. Is it not cute that we have braids? Eva made a doll for me to play with and for Ollie she made a little sailor boy. Bye, Clary

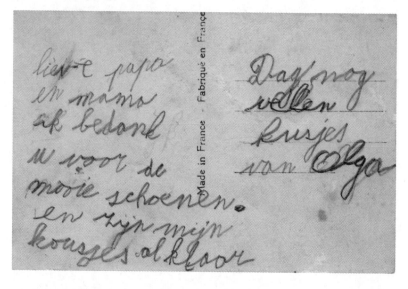

January, 1945
Dear Papa and Mama:
I want to thank you for the beautiful shoes. Are my stockings ready?
Bye, many kisses from Olga

~

In order to get some more food for us, Tante Nel would travel many miles out of town on her bike to get food from farmers by bartering our old clothes for food. Sometimes she was gone all day and night. She wanted to make sure we would not be hungry. We were happy that she took our old clothes with her and not our old shoes. We had to save our outgrown shoes and bring them to the Trading Bureau. The Trading Bureau was only open on Tuesdays and when Tante Nel left on a Sunday to go to the farmers, we knew she would be back on Tuesday to take us there.

We were so excited when Tante came back from the farm, impatient for her to empty her bicycle. We were always curious as to what was in her basket, even though most of the time there were only potatoes. She brought so many that we could hardly carry the heavy bag into the house. We would bring them to the kitchen, where Oma was waiting for us, to peel potatoes for our dinner. We didn't always feel like eating potatoes, but we were hungry and ate them anyhow. There was nothing else for us to eat.

We always looked forward to Saturdays, when Opa Wielaard would slaughter a chicken for our special Sunday dinner. It was the best meal of the week. It was difficult for him to do it by himself and he always asked us to help him hold the chicken while he tried to kill it, but we never wanted to, so he would ask Tante Nel. She knew it was the only way we would have a chicken on our plate on Sunday night. One time, she let go and we saw the chicken run around. Tante chased it but it got away, which we thought was funny. Although we felt sorry for the chicken, we were so hungry that we looked forward to Sunday when Oma would cook it for us.

Dear Papa:

How are you? The little chicken is walking in the garden. Tante Nel is chasing it. Our rabbits are getting big. One of the chickens laid an egg. I went with my viewing box and collected 25c. Papa, Ollie is sewing at the moment. She is making a bag for her doll. This morning we had to study again. If we continue to study we will be very smart, don't you think so? Bye, bye, Papa. Many kisses from Clary

~

Before bedtime we always played house. On one particular night in April 1945, after we had written to Pap for his birthday, we played house once again. This time, Ollie pretended to be Pap and I pretended to be Mam. All of a sudden, Ollie started crying and could not stop. I could tell Ollie really missed Mam and Pap; I think she was homesick and very lonely. I could understand why, having not seen our parents in almost three years. I was lonely too, but I had to be brave.

When she became really upset and wouldn't stop crying, it became very dangerous for all of us. I asked Tante Nel if she could take us to see Mam and Pap and she promised me that she would try but bringing both of us would be risky. She knew it would be hard since she didn't know, and was not to know, where my parents were hiding, but she said she would find a way. The next day, she asked her brother Pauw whether he could take Ollie to Mam and Pap. I would have liked to have gone too, however, I knew only one of us could go; it was dangerous enough.

When it got dark, Oom Pauw picked Ollie up. It was the safest time. I missed playing our imaginary games before bedtime and found it strange to fall asleep without my sister. I couldn't remember what Mam and Pap looked like, so I was anxious for Ollie to come back and tell me. I was sure they must have been so happy to see Ollie again. Secretly, I was still wishing I could have gone too.

When Ollie came back with Oom Pauw in the morning, I could tell right away that she seemed happier. She was smiling. Tante Nel had done the right thing. Ollie didn't cry any more and was happy to be back.

Papa:

From the clothing depot I received new slippers. Papa, I don't know what else to write, but I will make a drawing of the house where you live.

Many kisses, from Olga

~

Toward the end of April 1945, everyone was hoping that the war would soon be over. Five years of war was a very long time, most of Holland's population was starving, and the war effort had split apart many families.

It had been three years since I had seen my parents and I didn't even know if I would recognize them. We were anxious for the war to be over so we could be with them again. Even though Ollie had seen Mam and Pap a few weeks ago, we were both missing them and were longing to be with them again. Although we were happy with Tante Nel, we missed Mam and Pap's hugs and kisses.

Strangers at the Door

Finally, on May 5, 1945, we were liberated by the Canadian army. We were so excited to see Canadian soldiers on their Jeeps in Rotterdam. Our friends ran over to our house and screamed, "The war is over, the war is over!" They were jumping up and down and hugging us. They said that they were going to ask the Canadians if they could sit on one of their Jeeps and Tante Nel let us go with them, knowing we were safe. After we came back, we told Tante Nel that not only did we sit on a Jeep, but the soldiers had also given us chocolates and chewing gum while they took our picture. It was the most memorable and exciting day of our young lives!

And when we looked up we saw all kinds of planes and, out of the sky, packages were raining down. Each package contained food and our first piece of bread in such a long time. It was so delicious! Tante Nel called it, "Manna from heaven." She said that it was a miracle.

The war was finally over and we were free, but we still had not seen our parents and did not know if we were ever to see them. Then, there was such a loud knocking on our door. We were terrified – was this another house raid, which had frightened us the entire war?

No, this was to be the knock that would unite us forever! Tante Nel reassured us, telling us not to be afraid, that it was not a house raid and that the war was really over. She said that our parents were at the door but when we looked out, there stood two strangers. I saw a man carrying a large box, with a woman at his side. I wondered if they really were our parents. I didn't recognize them. In my memory, my dad was heavier and here stood two gaunt-looking people, two strangers. I was curious as to what was in such a large box.

Tante Nel told us that they really were our parents and we had to go home with them. Ollie recognized them more since she had visited Mam and Pap in April. I had seen a photo of what they looked like when we went into hiding, a picture Tante Nel kept hidden in her dresser, but it had been taken a long time ago and Tante had not shown it to us again because she didn't want us to miss them too much. Of course they looked so different; I hadn't seen them in three years.

At first, we didn't want to go home with Mam and Pap, but how could we not? They had purposely sent us away to save our lives. They were separated from us all these years while they were hiding elsewhere; we couldn't break their hearts. When they hugged me, it was a familiar hug. I knew then they were our parents. I had missed their hugs and kisses for almost three years.

It was difficult to say goodbye to our Tante Nel. We were so attached to her. We were going to miss her and we knew that she would miss us. In our hearts, we were hoping that it would never be a final goodbye, that she would always remain part of our family.

I still wondered why Pap was carrying such a large box, and then I remembered Oom Pauw telling us that Pap was making a surprise for us. Was this it? Why did he bring us a present? He did not have to. We now had our present, our parents. It was the best present of all.

Although it was time to go home, we no longer had a home of our own. We had to share our house with others who had also lost their homes. We were given temporary shared housing provided by the Jewish Relief Agency. We moved to a large house in Overschie, a suburb of Rotterdam, that had been occupied by the Nazis during the war.

Once we arrived there, Pap had us open the box that he had brought with him. It contained a beautiful dollhouse with many rooms, complete with furniture he had made out of matchboxes. It must have taken him a long time. I told Ollie to be very careful not to break the furniture, which was so fragile, but Pap told her not to worry and that this beautiful dollhouse was for both of us, to make up for all those years that we had nothing to play with.

We were so busy playing with our dollhouse that we didn't pay any attention to our new surroundings, our temporary home. Ollie and I didn't really know the difference. We had lived in so many different places that this house didn't stand out from all the others. We just knew that we were finally home with Mam and Pap and that they would never leave us again.

In Overschie, we lived on the main floor, sharing the house with a very eccentric lady, Mrs. Werthmuller-Von Elk. Before the war, she was the lady-in-waiting for Queen Wilhelmina. Once the war broke out and the queen left for England, she lost her position and escaped to the East Indies. Now she lived upstairs, alone, with her parrot. Ollie and I always enjoyed visiting Mrs. Werthmuller, although her parrot swore at us and called us dirty names. Mrs. Werthmuller had brought back two special paper marionettes from the East Indies and she never minded us playing with them even though they were very fragile.

For two years, Ollie and I had lived in such a small basement apartment that this house seemed tremendous and we had such fun. We went up into the attic and found all types of German stamps in albums. Mam had told us not to touch anything, but we didn't listen this time, so we looked around, curious, and walked from room to room to see what else we could find.

A few days later, my dad went to see Tante Nel. He was so full of emotion. It was hard for him to express his gratitude. While he was in hiding, he had made a special plaque with the following inscription: 1943–1945. *Thank you for all your care while we were hiding in your home.* He was hoping to give it to her after the war, in the hope that we all survived. As soon as he gave it to her, she hung it in a very special place, on her living room wall. Even in later years, when she moved to a retirement home, the plaque hung on her wall there, until the day she passed away.

Within that same week, the entire neighbourhood in Rotterdam Zuid (South) honoured Tante Nel with a party where they gave her flowers and gifts. It was then that Nel realized that the whole neighbourhood, and our friends, had known that we were Jewish and that everyone had kept quiet. Although she had always liked and trusted her neighbours, she had sometimes doubted that she could have trusted all of them. Now, she felt that they, not she, were the special ones. By not betraying us, they were heroes.

When a young man came from the local newspaper to interview Tante Nel about her experiences, at first she said no. She had been missing us, she told us later, and didn't want to talk about it. However, the young man insisted, telling her she was special and that her story needed to be published, so she relented. The next morning, she cut out the following article and kept it in her diary:

"The Hunger Winter: Everyone who went through this period had their own experiences, as did Mrs. Van Woudenberg from Rotterdam. In 1943, two small little girls came to her house, ages five and seven. She had to face this totally alone during the Hunger Winter. The last memory she has of the various trips to obtain some food she explained as follows:

On the third of May I left with my bicycle and walked from early in the morning until 7:00 at night to get some more food for the girls. On the fourth of May I returned, my bicycle packed totally full. I was so tired; I have never been so tired. Once I arrived home, there was only one thing to do, find my bed and rest. When I awoke I heard a tremendous noise on the street. The girls looked outside and screamed out loud, "We are free – the war is over!"

I almost did not care since I was so terribly tired.

~

We were extremely lucky to have survived in hiding; thousands of Jews were betrayed by Holland's many collaborators. Before the war, Holland's Jewish population was approximately 140,000; only 30,000 survived, most in hiding. Of the slightly more than 100,000 Dutch Jews who were sent from the Westerbork transit camp to the death camps and concentration camps – mainly Auschwitz and Sobibor, but also Theresienstadt, Bergen-Belsen, Dachau and Mauthausen – merely five thousand or so survived.

In the whole of Europe, among six million Jewish deaths, 1.5 million children did not survive. In Holland, approximately 5,000 children went into hiding and only 3,500 survived. After the war, some of these children were not immediately returned to their rightful parents because of a law that the united Dutch resistance group proposed to the Dutch government-in-exile in London in 1944.

In short, the law, which came into effect soon after liberation in May 1945, said that Dutch Jewish children who were in hiding from the Nazis should not be returned to their Jewish parents if they were not claimed within one month after the war, and should remain either with their foster parents or under the guardianship of a war orphan commission. The law implied that, as these children were raised for months and even years by Christian foster families and taught the Christian religion, it was much easier for them to remain Christian rather than be returned to their Jewish family, whom they may not remember.

If a Jewish parent or parents demanded their children back, they had to defend their claim to their own children before a committee. They had to prove that they were able to raise their children properly, that they had a house and the financial means to do so, and had practised the Jewish religion for the last six months. In the case of Jewish orphans, the committee, comprised mostly of non-Jews, made often ill-informed decisions about whether the child should be placed in foster care or with extended family members. How lucky we were to have been with our Tante Nel, who gave us up so willingly.

In one of our letters to Mam and Pap while we were hiding, we had asked if we could have a dog when the war was over.

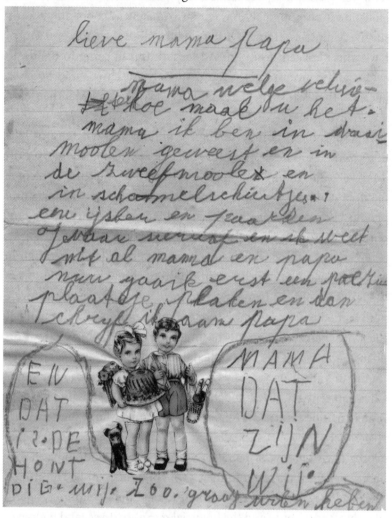

Dear Mama and Papa:

Mama, how are you? I have been in the merry-go-round and on the carousel with horses. The rest I do not know. I do not know what to write. I am pasting a picture on the bottom of the letter, which I have cut out. You can see it has two children with a dog, that is us. And that is the dog we are wishing for and hope to have.

Many kisses, Clary

With the war over, Mam and Pap kept their promise. We were given our very special little dog, whom we named Scotty.

Claire (left) with her sister, Ollie, and their new dog.

Now it was time for us to go to a regular public school. Since our only education had been home schooling, there was a problem as to which grade we should be placed in. I remember walking to school with our dog, Scotty, being nervous and wondering what it was going to be like to be in a real school with other children.

The teacher placed me in Grade 1, which was Ollie's class. I already knew arithmetic, as well as being able to read and write, so by the end of the day the teacher said I really belonged in the third grade. The following day, I marched into my new Grade 3 classroom. It felt strange to be in a classroom with other children.

For almost three years after the war, we lived in Overschie, in our temporary house. Most of our possessions were gone, as was our home, our family's factory and many of our parents' friends as well as most of our extended family. The Nazis had taken everything away and we doubted that anything was going to be returned. Although there were many details to look after, our parents realized how lucky they were for the four of us to have survived.

We wondered about my grandparents – were they still alive? In our hearts, we believed that they were not so lucky, but we were still hoping that they would return. Unfortunately, after waiting three more years, the reality set in. In 1948 our family received notification from the Red Cross that Mam's parents, my grandparents, had died in Auschwitz in 1943. Pap also found out that his parents, brother and sister, as well as practically all of his extended family, with the exception of his eighteen-year-old nephew, had not survived.

My parents were living with the constant memory of the Holocaust and they wanted us to leave Holland and try to leave those memories behind. That same year, in 1948, my Dad arranged for our passports to take us anywhere by obtaining a visitor's permit. He didn't want to wait for immigration papers again; he remembered very well how we were refused in 1939. He wanted our family to find a better life and a new beginning, leaving our memories as well as our few remaining possessions behind.

Although we wanted to leave as soon as possible, it took three more years for my parents to decide where to go. We didn't have too many choices. Fortunately, we saw an opportunity in Canada and in 1951 we made our final decision to leave. This time, with our visitor's permit, we knew we could never be refused.

On March 15, 1951, we left Holland and went to the land of our Canadian liberators. Five years later, in 1956, the year I was married, we received our Canadian citizenship and became proud Canadians. We had found a new beginning and never looked back.

Epilogue

In 1967, about six months after the Six-Day War, my husband, Seymour, and I travelled to Israel. As I stood beside Seymour at the Wailing Wall on our first day in Jerusalem, it was the last day of Chanukah. When I looked up, I witnessed the most unforgettable sight. There were eight oil vessels burning on top of the Wall. It was the first time, the first Chanukah since Jerusalem was reunited. Not only was this an extremely emotional experience, but I was also so grateful to have been spared the atrocities of the Holocaust.

I could only think that, as a survivor of the Holocaust, it was a miracle to be standing here in Jerusalem, Israel, with my husband by my side. I was so proud to be Jewish and considered myself very fortunate to be able to raise our three children, Dianne, Jeffrey and Jacqueline, in total freedom, as Jews and not as Christians, due to the courage of my parents and to the courage of Tante Nel.

The very next day, Seymour and I went to Yad Vashem where the righteous gentiles, formally called the Righteous Among the Nations, are recognized. As we walked along the many paths and I looked at the various names, I did not have to be reminded of how our Tante Nel had risked her life to save us. Tante Nel deserved to have her place among the righteous. She had to be recognized.

Upon our return from Israel, my parents started making all the necessary arrangements to have Tante Nel recognized at Yad Vashem.

However, it took several years to get all the documentation in place. On July 25, 1979, Tante Nel was finally given her well-deserved honour. She was unable to travel to Israel, so the Israeli Ambassador in Holland bestowed the special medal on her as well as a certificate that reads: "Who under perilous circumstances risked her life to save Jews during the Holocaust, has hereby been given a special Award of Merit."

Our son, Jeffrey, planted a tree on the Avenue of the Righteous at Yad Vashem in her honour. A simple plaque bears her name: Nel Van Woudenberg, Holland. It is there for all to see how our Tante Nel made a difference by risking her life to save us. She was our hero. The Talmud teaches, "He who saves one life saves the world." Tante Nel saved an entire generation of our family. Isaiah, verse 56:5, says, "I shall give them a place in my home and an everlasting name so they will not perish." Many times, the heroes in our survivor stories are forgotten; the story of Nel Van Woudenberg, our Dutch rescuer, a Righteous Gentile who risked her life in order to save both me and my sister, must be told.

After we immigrated to Canada, during our yearly visits with Tante Nel, she would recount the days between 1943 and 1945 when she was hiding both me and my sister. She had written a partial diary and took a number of photographs during that time, and I was able to weave them into her complete story as it was told to me. At no time did she ever consider herself to be a hero.

~

In the spring of 1942, Nel married a man named Kees. He had wanted to start a family right away, but Nel wasn't interested; she came to see her husband as a rather demanding man who was only interested in himself and his pigeons; he would retreat into his pigeon coop for hours and sometimes for days on end. Since it was wartime, there was a possibility he would be called up to work in Germany. Nel decided it was not the right time to raise a family.

In October 1942, when Kees was called up, he was pleased to be going to a German work camp. He had always wanted to be needed and never felt that his life had been fulfilled. He was an unhappy man, so off he went without regret.

After Kees left for Germany, Nel's life was very peaceful and quiet. She felt somewhat relieved that her husband was far away. She made sure to clean his pigeon coop in case he came back early. Although the days were long, with her parents and her younger brother, Jan, next door, she always had something to do and was never lonely.

Her two older brothers, Leen and Pauw, asked her for help many times when they were working very late hours. Nel had never asked them where they worked and had absolutely no idea they belonged to the Resistance, who mostly met at night. She had never questioned them; it was not her style.

In April 1943, on a rainy and miserable day, Nel received a call from her brother Pauw, asking if she had room for two little girls for a couple of days. He didn't give her many details, only that they were five and seven years old and that he had to bring them back with him. At first, Nel didn't know what to make of it. She wondered why her brother sounded so passionate. Did he know the girls? When Nel pressed him a bit, he told her that both he and Leen had joined the Resistance and that they had been approached by a Jewish family of four, the Friedbergs, to find a Christian home. The Resistance couldn't hide the entire family together and had advised them to separate. After her brother told her of their plight, and the betrayal the girls had experienced at their first hiding place, Nel, being a good Christian, knew that she had to save us; she could not stand by.

Nel faced several problems. What would she tell her neighbours? Her brother told her not to worry, that the girls' parents had prepared them very well with an alibi and that they would say they were related and call her Tante Nel. They were to be her nieces, family. Pauw could only tell Nel that the parents were hiding in the same city, but could not reveal the address; it was too dangerous.

Gradually, Nel became attached to us, but had to be careful not to show us too much affection; she didn't want us to forget that we had our own parents. Once, after we had been separated from our parents for almost six months, Pauw arranged for our parents to come for a short visit. I didn't remember this, but Nel told me we were waiting for them in the front room of her house and that in her hurry, she had forgotten to close the door to the hall. Ollie, who was only five years old, noticed and knew she had to protect us – if someone had come in and seen all of us together, it could have spelled disaster. She told Tante Nel, "It is getting drafty in here, you better close the door." Nel was amazed that Ollie knew how to spot a dangerous situation.

Nel always followed the same routine for our home schooling – reading and writing in the morning, followed by arithmetic in the afternoon. She bought us books to read before bedtime.

It would have been impossible to feed us with the wartime rations, as only one card was given per family. Because the Resistance had made duplicate ration cards, Nel was able to provide food, but she had to be careful not to buy too much when grocery shopping. Somebody might notice; anyone could be a collaborator.

Nel was surprised that we adjusted so well. She insisted we write to our parents regularly so as not to forget them, and she was always careful that we not get too used to her. Nel was surprised that we didn't seem to be lonely or cry. She found it rather remarkable that we never argued or fought with each other, simply because we had been told not to. She reminded me that when Ollie got a bit teary, I immediately calmed her down.

During the Hunger Winter, Nel worked so hard to get us food. On May 3, 1945, two days before liberation, Nel had travelled such a long distance to get food for us. The next day, she was so happy to be home, and could not wait to get into bed. She was exhausted. She was soon awoken by strange noises; they seemed to be coming from the street. That is when we came into her bedroom screaming, "The war is over!" She looked outside and saw it was true – there were planes overhead, Canadian soldiers on their Jeeps.

Nel was aware that, at any moment, our parents would be at the door. Her brother Pauw would soon be on his way with the Friedbergs and she had to face the fact that she would lose us. She had formed such an attachment to us and she also didn't know how we would react, whether we would want to leave, but she knew she had to let us go. It was going to be difficult and she would miss us, but our place was with our parents.

When our parents came to the door that day, Nel said that we didn't seem excited. We told Nel that we didn't know them, that they were strangers. Nevertheless, we knew we had to leave with them. When we threw our arms around Nel to say goodbye, she could not control her tears. It was the first time that she became emotional.

That first week, she missed us and was not in the mood to celebrate the end of the war. When my father came and gave her the thank-you plaque, thanking her profusely, he said we would never forget her and that she would always play a big part in our lives. Being a modest woman, she had never felt she deserved all this praise. She felt that what she had done was nothing special.

After liberation, Nel knew that Kees was on his way home and that she would have to face reality. She had not thought about him throughout the war and was not looking forward to his return. Her life had been so peaceful without him, but when Kees arrived, he was happy to be back. He had missed both home and Nel. Nel knew she had to give him a chance and start over. They decided to raise a family and one year later Nel gave birth to a son, Aat. She adored him and was pleased to finally have her own family. Soon after, our family visited and told her we were hoping to leave Holland soon but would always stay in touch.

One year after the birth of their son, her relationship ended in divorce. Two years later, Nel married a man named Koos and he, too, became part of our family. Within five years, Nel and Koos became the parents of two more children, daughters they named Paula and Nellie. They were very proud parents and were a very happy couple.

Eventually, they had seven wonderful grandchildren. Paula, their eldest daughter, had three beautiful sons, their son, Aat, had two girls and a boy, and Nellie had a lovely daughter, Yolanda. When Paula was diagnosed with lung cancer, Nel was devastated but never complained about her lot either to me or to Ollie when we called.

Nel saved all the correspondence from our family in Canada, was always thrilled when Ollie and I came to visit, and proudly displayed our wedding photos on her mantle. In June 1974, when Nel and Koos received an invitationto to the bar mitzvah of my son, Jeffrey, Nel told me that they were flattered and excited, although neither had ever been in a plane and were nervous. She wrote about this trip in her diary, which I now have, describing the clouds as resembling "mounds of whipped cream."

On June 15, the day of Jeffrey's bar mitzvah at Beth Sholom synagogue, Nel wrote in her diary, *The synagogue was packed. It was an experience to be recorded or taped. After the service, which lasted roughly an hour, the rabbi gave his sermon. He spoke about the Woudenberg family, where Jeffrey's mother and aunt were in hiding. He could not stop talking about us. We then had to stand up. There was a thunderous applause and we were given a standing ovation. Koos was so emotional that he reached for a handkerchief, not being able to stop the flow of tears. We were asked to say a few words, but it was just too difficult.*

In 1975, Nel returned to Canada to celebrate my nephew Ronnie's bar mitzvah. Unfortunately, Koos was not well enough to travel; sadly, he passed away shortly after.

In 1979, as I've mentioned, Nel was awarded the righteous designation. Nel told me that she was awestruck, feeling that she did not deserve the honour, but was so grateful to our family.

Years later, Nel's daughter Nellie divorced her husband. When Nellie's daughter, Yolanda, reached her teen years, Nellie, as a single mother, found it difficult to raise her daughter. Nel decided to bring up her granddaughter, knowing it was in her daughter's best interests. Much later on, Yolanda rented an apartment in the same complex as

Nel and was able to return the favour by taking care of her elderly grandmother.

In 1995, Ollie and her daughter Jennifer visited Nel as a surprise. And once a year, for many years, Seymour and I went to visit. After Nel's daughter Paula passed away and could no longer act as a Dutch translator for Seymour, I continued to visit on my own, as Nel could not speak or understand English too well and it would have been too difficult for me to translate all our conversations. Nel told me that it was the highlight of her life to reminisce and spend time with both me and Ollie.

In 2002, on the occasion of Yolanda's upcoming wedding, Nel sent invitations to us, her "family" in Canada, with whom she had such a special bond. Ollie was unable to go at that time so my daughter Dianne and I made the trip. Dianne was so pleased to be able to meet this very special and humble family and take part in their celebration.

A few years later, Nel moved into a retirement home. When Ollie and her husband, Warner, visited her, they saw that the plaque that Pap had made so long ago was, even there, hanging on the wall of her room. They knew Nel would never forget us. Unfortunately, it was the very last visit. In 2006, at age ninety-three, Nel passed away. Ollie and I had stayed in touch with her for sixty years and it was an unbelievable loss; we felt as though we had lost our lifeline, our special caregiver and our other mother. We had never been able to repay her for saving our lives.

We knew that she was grateful we had always stayed in touch. We will never forget her and will always remember her as our definition of a hero: it was she, an ordinary person, who under very difficult circumstances had done an extraordinary deed. She had not only saved two little girls, but she had also saved their future generations.

Our Family

According to our family's genealogy, our parents, grandparents and great-grandparents were all born and lived in Holland as Dutch citizens for centuries, going back to the Golden Age. Nevertheless, during the war they were considered Jewish and not Dutch. Most of our extended family were persecuted by the Nazis and lost their lives simply because they were Jewish.

Several years ago, when Seymour and I visited De Waag, the former Jewish Museum in Amsterdam, we admired two ark covers from a synagogue in Middelburg – where my mother was born – that had been hidden from the Nazis. This was the same synagogue in which my mother, as well as her ancestors, had prayed. Unfortunately, today it's merely a monument of a glorious past.

MY MOTHER'S FAMILY

My mother, Sophia Aaltjen Cohen, was born on October 7, 1909, in Middelburg.

My maternal great-grandfather, Joseph Drilsma, was born on November 18, 1852, in Middelburg. My maternal great-grandmother was Aaltjen Oppenheimer.

My maternal grandparents were Jacob Israel Cohen, born in Middelburg on July 10, 1884, and Clara Drilsma, who was born in

The Hague on October 7, 1884. They were married on September 16, 1908, and they both died in Auschwitz in February 1943.

My maternal great-great-great grandfather, Jonas Lazarus, was born in 1699 and died in Emden, Germany, in 1773, where his gravestone still exists. He was married to Klaartje Arons, who passed away in 1741. Jonas Lazarus worked in the lumber business, owned quite a bit of property and was one of the richest Jews in Germany. In a book written by Jan Lokers about the influential Jews of Emden from 1530 to 1806, it is noted that Jonas Lazarus ordered cargo to be shipped, at his expense, from Sweden to Amsterdam and Emden. Lazarus was a patriarch who had a large family and, of his six to nine descendants, many had eleven children. My great-grandmother had eight siblings. It is interesting to note that not only were they a wealthy family, but they were also extremely active in the Jewish community and the synagogue, as both *mohels* and *chazzans*. One of the descendants was the famous painter Jozef Israëls.

MY FATHER'S FAMILY

My father, Rudolph David Friedberg, was born on April 7, 1908, in Rotterdam.

My paternal grandparents were Jossel Friedberg and Olga Isaacson, both born in Libau. They had three children, Benno, Fanny and Rudolph. Olga died in 1935. In 1938 Jossel married Elfriede Huppert, born in Beuthen on November 5, 1883. They first lived in Scheveningen and later in Amsterdam. Jossel David Friedberg was a retired works manager. He helped his son Benno with resistance work. In October 1942 they were both caught in Amsterdam and deported to Sobibor via Westerbork. They died in Sobibor on July 23, 1943.

THE LAMENT OF MY DAD, A HOLOCAUST SURVIVOR
"Does liberation mean freedom?"

Freedom from remembering or questioning? NEVER!

1945 – 1950:

I see people in trouble –	I remember
I see fireworks –	I remember
I see and hear airplanes –	I remember
I hear of assassinations –	I remember
I hear of child abuse –	I remember
I hear of separation –	I remember
I hear and see discrimination –	I remember
I hear of starvation –	I remember
I have to sign a petition –	I remember
I hear of immigration refusal –	I remember

1951: Finally we are in a new country – Canada. We are free.

My family is happy –	I do not want to remember.
I am building a new life for my family –	I am happy,
	I do not want to remember.

My children are happy and settled in their new country,
Canada –   I am happy,
                                                  I do not want to remember.
My children attend public school –   I am happy,
                                                  I do not want to remember.
I am making a living for my family –   I am happy,
                                                  I do not want to remember.

But, in the twilight of my years as my health fails me, I begin to question:

When did my parents perish?   I question.
How much did they suffer?   I question.
Where and how did they die?   I question.
Why did they not survive?   I question.

And…

Was it courage or merely luck that my children, wife and I survived?

However, when death is on my doorstep, perhaps God will have the answers.
My only hope is that I will be reunited with my lost family.

Then, and only then, will I be at peace at last.

Written in honour of my dad
Claire Baum
April 27, 1995

Glossary

Auschwitz (German; in Polish, Oświęcim) A Nazi concentration
  camp complex in German-occupied Poland about 50 kilometres
  from Krakow, on the outskirts of the town of Oświęcim, built between 1940 and 1942. The largest camp complex established by
  the Nazis, Auschwitz contained three main camps: Auschwitz I, a
  concentration camp; Auschwitz II (Birkenau), a death camp that
  used gas chambers to commit mass murder; and Auschwitz III
  (also called Monowitz or Buna), which provided slave labour for
  an industrial complex. In 1942, the Nazis began to deport Jews
  from almost every country in Europe to Auschwitz, where they
  were selected for slave labour or for death in the gas chambers. In
  mid-January 1945, close to 60,000 inmates were sent on a death
  march, leaving behind only a few thousand inmates who were liberated by the Soviet army on January 27, 1945. It is estimated that
  1.1 million people were murdered in Auschwitz, approximately 90
  per cent of whom were Jewish; other victims included Polish prisoners, Roma and Soviet prisoners of war.
Chanukah (also Hanukah; Hebrew; dedication) An eight-day festival
  of lights, usually celebrated in December, that commemorates the
  victory of the Jews against the Syrian-Greek empire in the second century BCE. The festival is celebrated with the lighting of an
  eight-branched candelabrum called a menorah, or chanukiah, in

remembrance of the rededication of the Temple in Jerusalem and the miracle of one day's worth of oil burning for eight days.

chazzan (Hebrew) A cantor who leads a synagogue congregation in songful prayer. The *chazzan* might be professionally trained or a member of the congregation.

Commission for War Foster Children (in Dutch, Commissie voor Oorlogspleegkinderen; abbreviation OPK) A state committee established in 1945 by former members of the Dutch Resistance to decide the placement of Jewish war orphans. The commission passed a law that if a Jewish parent did not return to claim their child within one month after the end of the war, children who had been in hiding with gentile families came under the OPK's jurisdiction. The commission, which comprised a minority of Jewish members, decided where to place Jewish orphans based on what they perceived to be the children's best interests, in many cases determining that the children should remain with their Christian foster families. Of the approximately 1,300 orphaned Dutch-Jewish children who came before the commission, between 400–500 were placed with non-Jewish families. The OPK was dissolved in 1949.

Hunger Winter The term used for the famine in the German-occupied western Netherlands during the winter of 1944–1945. In retaliation for the national railway strike coordinated by the Dutch government-in-exile and the Allies in an effort to stop the movement of German troops, Germany banned food transports to the area. Although the embargo was lifted after six weeks, the combination of a harsh winter, frozen-over canals, the lack of train transport and the destruction of bridges meant that food transports were completely cut off from the region, resulting in approximately 20,000 deaths from starvation.

Kristallnacht (German; Night of Broken Glass) A series of antisemitic attacks instigated by the Nazi leadership that were perpetrated in Germany and the recently-annexed territories of Austria and the Sudetenland on November 9 and 10, 1938. During Kristall-nacht, ninety-one Jews were murdered, and between 25,000 and 30,000 Jewish men were arrested and deported to concentration camps. More than two hundred synagogues were burned down, and thousands of Jewish homes and businesses were ransacked, their windows shattered, giving Kristallnacht its name. This attack is considered a decisive turning point in the Nazis' systematic persecution of Jews.

mohel A Jewish person trained in ritual circumcision (removal of the foreskin of the penis), who performs a bris eight days after a baby is born. A bris is Judaism's religious ceremony to welcome male infants into the covenant between God and the Children of Israel.

Mussert, Anton (1894–1946) One of the founders of the fascist Dutch National Socialist Movement (NSB) and its leader during World War II. Mussert, who was given the title "Leader of the Dutch People," worked under Nazi official Arthur Seyss-Inquart, collaborating with Nazi policies against the Dutch-Jewish population. In May 1945, Mussert was arrested and found guilty of war crimes; he was executed near The Hague in May 1946. *See also* National Socialist Movement; Seyss-Inquart, Arthur.

National Socialist Movement (in Dutch, Nationaal-Socialistische Beweging; abbreviation NSB) A far-right fascist political party established in 1931 that gained power leading up to and during World War II. The ideology and policies of the NSB were modelled on Italian fascism and German National Socialism (Nazism) but did not become expressly antisemitic until the mid-1930s, when the party reached 50,000 members. During the German occupation, NSB was the only legal political party in the Netherlands, and its paramilitary police force was involved in rounding up Jews.

Nationale Jeugdstorm (Dutch; National Youth Storm; NJS) A nationalistic Dutch youth group – modelled on Germany's fascist Hitlerjugend (Hitler Youth) organization – that was affiliated with the larger Dutch National Socialist Movement (NSB). The Jeugdstorm was founded in 1934 and had about 15,000 members by 1942. The youth, aged ten to eighteen, participated in sport activities and watched propaganda films about Hitler; unlike the Hitler Youth, they were not engaged in military action. *See also* National Socialist Movement.

razzia (German; raid) A mass arrest of Jews who were then sent to do forced labour, deported to Nazi camps or killed.

Resistance (Netherlands) The collective term for the various different factions that operated in opposition to the Nazis during their occupation of the Netherlands. Resistance took various forms – helping to create forged documents for Jews; solidarity strikes by non-Jewish Dutch workers to protest the deportation of Jews; underground newspapers; gathering intelligence information; and helping Jews into hiding. At least four different organizations were dedicated solely to hiding Jewish children.

Righteous Among the Nations A title given by Yad Vashem, the World Holocaust Remembrance Center in Jerusalem, to honour non-Jews who risked their lives to help save Jews during the Holocaust. A commission was established in 1963 to award the title. If a person fits certain criteria and the story is carefully checked, the honouree is awarded with a medal and certificate and is commemorated on the Wall of Honour at the Garden of the Righteous in Jerusalem.

Seyss-Inquart, Arthur (1892–1946) An Austrian Nazi official who served as chancellor of Austria in 1938, a deputy in the Nazi General Government of Poland in 1939, and *Reichskommisar* (imperial commissioner) of the Netherlands from 1940 until the end of the war. Seyss-Inquart, an ardent antisemite, oversaw the civilian administration of the country, establishing anti-Jewish laws and a forced labour service, and overseeing the execution of opponents to the regime. After the war, he was tried and found guilty as a war criminal during the Nuremberg Trials, and was sentenced to hanging in October 1946.

Shabbat (Hebrew; Sabbath; in Yiddish, Shabbes, Shabbos) The weekly day of rest beginning Friday at sunset and ending Saturday at nightfall, ushered in by the lighting of candles on Friday evening and the recitation of blessings over wine and challah (egg bread). A day of celebration as well as prayer, it is customary to eat three festive meals, attend synagogue services and refrain from doing any work or travelling.

Six-Day War The armed conflict between Israel and its neighbouring states of Egypt, Jordan and Syria that took place June 5–10, 1967. In response to growing tensions between Israel and its neighbouring Arab countries, Israel launched a pre-emptive attack. In the days that followed, Israeli forces drove the Arab armies back and occupied the Sinai Peninsula, Gaza Strip, West Bank and Golan Heights. Israel also reunited Jerusalem, the eastern half of which Jordan had controlled since the 1948 Arab-Israeli war.

SS (abbreviation of Schutzstaffel; Defence Corps) The elite police force of the Nazi regime that was responsible for security and for the enforcement of Nazi racial policies, including the implementation of the Final Solution — a euphemistic term referring to the Nazis' plan to systematically murder Europe's Jewish population. The SS was established in 1925 as Adolf Hitler's elite bodyguard unit, and under the direction of Heinrich Himmler, its membership grew from 280 in 1929 to 52,000 when the Nazis came to power in 1933, and to nearly a quarter of a million on the eve of World War II. SS recruits were screened for their racial purity and had to prove their "Aryan" lineage. The SS ran the concentration and death camps and also established the Waffen-SS, its own military division that was independent of the German army.

St. Nikolaas Day The annual December 5 Christian holiday of Sinterklaas in the Netherlands that celebrates the feast day of Saint Nicholas, who was revered as a gift giver and miracle worker.

Star of David (in Hebrew, Magen David) The six-pointed star that is the most recognizable symbol of Judaism. During World War II, Jews in Nazi-occupied areas were frequently forced to wear a badge or armband with the Star of David on it as an identifying mark of their lesser status and to single them out as targets for persecution.

Westerbork A transit and internment camp that was located in northeastern Netherlands in the province of Drenthe, near the town of Westerbork. Established by the Dutch government in October 1939 to hold Jewish refugees, the camp came under German authority during the occupation. Between July 1942 and September 1944, close to 100,000 Jews were interned at Westerbork and, on more than one hundred transports, were deported to the Nazi death camps and concentration camps of Auschwitz, Sobibor, Theresienstadt and Bergen-Belsen. Canadian forces liberated the remaining people from Westerbork on April 12, 1945.

Yad Vashem Israel's official Holocaust memorial centre and the world's largest collection of information on the Holocaust, established in 1953. Yad Vashem, the World Holocaust Remembrance Center, is dedicated to commemoration, research, documentation and education about the Holocaust. The Yad Vashem complex in Jerusalem includes museums, sculptures, exhibitions, research centres and the Garden of the Righteous Among the Nations.

Photographs

1 & 2 Claire Baum's paternal grandparents, Jossel (Joseph) and Olga (née Isaacson) Friedberg.

3 & 4 Jacob and Clara (née Drilsma) Cohen, Claire's maternal grandparents.

Wedding day of Sophia and Rudolph Friedberg, Claire's parents. Rotterdam, July 26, 1934.

1

2

3

1 Claire with her mother, Sophia, strolling with newborn Ollie. Rotterdam, circa 1937.

2 Claire and her sister, Ollie, dressed up for Aunt Rosa and Uncle Joe's wedding.

3 In Dutch costume in the village of Volendam, circa 1940.

1 Claire and Ollie.

2 Claire's family with her maternal grandparents. Back row, left to right: Claire's mother, Sophia, Grandmother Clara and Claire's father, Rudolph. In front: Ollie, Grandfather Jacob and Claire.

3 The Friedberg family before the war.

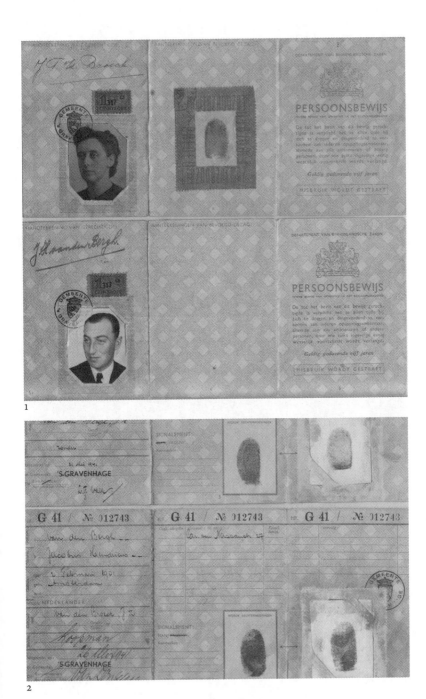

1 & 2 Claire's parents' falsified identification cards, circa 1941.

Rotterdam, December 20th. 1949

No. 20.009.S.C.
Type MS/M.
Ref. SOCIALE COMMISSIE.

TO WHOM IT MAY CONCERN.

This is to certify, that

R U D O L P H   D A V I D   F R I E D B E R G,

(7.-4.-1908) Rotterdam, Burgemeester Meineszlaan 67
joined our underground resistance movement during the
war 1940 - 1945 and rended valuable service to this
country.

Sociale Commissie der N.F.R.
v/h. Voormalig Verzet
De Sercretaris:

(M. Beckbach)

The document issued by the Dutch National Federal Council of the Resistance to confirm that Claire's father participated in the underground resistance during the war.

1 Claire (far right) and Ollie, beside her, with Jopie and Tante Kor, the first family they were in hiding with during the war. Soestduinen, 1942.
2 Claire (left) and Ollie soon after arriving at Tante Nel's, their new hiding place in Rotterdam. 1943.
3 Ollie and Claire (left) with Tante Nel, circa 1944.
4 In the Wielaards' chicken coop with their rabbits. Rotterdam, 1944.

1 Liberation day in Rotterdam, May 5, 1945. Claire and Ollie are seated on the Jeep, behind the stilts.

2 Claire (right) and Ollie with two of their liberators from the Canadian Army. May 5, 1945.

Claire and Ollie with their mother, Sophia, on the doorstep of their temporary
home after the war. Overschie, 1945–46.

Claire and Seymour's wedding day. Toronto, October 28, 1956.

1

2

3

1 Celebrating Jeffrey's bar mitzvah. Back row, left to right: Nel, Koos, Seymour,
   Claire, and her parents, Sophia and Rudolph. In front, left to right: Claire's
   mother-in-law, Ray Baum, and Claire's children, Dianne, Jeffrey and Jacqueline.
   June 1974.
2 Wedding photo of Tante Nel (Nel Van Woudenberg) and her husband, Koos. Rotterdam, 1946.
3 Nel and Koos in Toronto for the bar mitzvah of Claire's son, Jeffrey. June 1974.

1   Certificate from Yad Vashem recognizing Nel Van Woudenberg as Righteous
    Among the Nations. Jerusalem, July 25, 1979.

2   The special plaque that Claire's father made for Tante Nel while he was in hiding,
    thanking her for keeping Claire and Ollie safe during the war.

3   Nel's plaque on the Avenue of the Righteous at Yad Vashem, Jerusalem.

1 Nel Van Woudenberg, circa 2000.
2 Claire visiting Nel on the occasion of Nel's granddaughter Yolanda's wedding.
   Rotterdam, 2002.
3 The Baum-Friedberg family, circa 2007. Back row, left to right: Claire's grand-
   daughters Laura and Kara; her son-in-law Grant and daughter Dianne; her
   daughter Jacqueline and son-in-law Michael; daughter-in-law, Tali, and son,
   Jeffrey, holding his son Jonathan. In front, left to right: Claire's mother, Sophia
   Friedberg; Claire and her granddaughter Courtney; Seymour and granddaughter
   Jenna; granddaughter Blair; granddaughter Dana; and grandson Daniel.

Ontario

In recognition and appreciation of

CLAIRE BAUM

Holocaust Survivor

May 3, 2012

*On behalf of the Government of Ontario, I am honoured
to join Ontarians provincewide in paying solemn tribute to you for
your profound courage, strength and determination.*

*Few can fully comprehend the unspeakable suffering,
cruelty and inhumanity that you and your fellow Holocaust
survivors witnessed and endured.*

*Yours is a remarkable story, one that serves as a
compelling reminder of our obligation — as a society and as
individuals — to learn from the lessons of history, to be vigilant against all forms
of hatred and intolerance, and to embrace inclusiveness and
diversity — in the laws of our land and in our hearts.*

*You are a role model, a hero, a true survivor.
Please accept my personal best wishes.*

Dalton McGuinty
Premier

Claire Baum's certificate of recognition from the Ontario government and the Canadian Society for Yad Vashem, given in appreciation for her many achievements and her contribution to Holocaust education.

Claire Baum accepting her certificate with then Ontario premier Dalton
McGuinty (left), Minister of Citizenship and Immigration Charles Sousa (centre)
and MPP York Centre Monte Kwinter (right). May 3, 2012.

Index

Fondation
Azrieli
Foundation

The Azrieli Foundation was established in 1989 to realize and extend the philanthropic vision of David J. Azrieli, C.M., C.Q., M.Arch. The Foundation's mission is to support a wide spectrum of initiatives in education and research. The Azrieli Foundation is an active supporter of programs in the fields of education, the education of architects, scientific and medical research, and the arts. The Azrieli Foundation's many initiatives include: the Holocaust Survivor Memoirs Program, which collects, preserves, publishes and distributes the written memoirs of survivors in Canada; the Azrieli Institute for Educational Empowerment, an innovative program successfully working to keep at-risk youth in school; the Azrieli Fellows Program, which promotes academic excellence and leadership on the graduate level at Israeli universities; the Azrieli Music Project, which celebrates and fosters the creation of high-quality new Jewish orchestral music; and the Azrieli Neurodevelopmental Research Program, which supports advanced research on neurodevelopmental disorders, particularly Fragile X and Autism Spectrum Disorders.